Corporate Governance
in
Thailand

Corporate
Governance
in
Thailand

edited by
Sakulrat Montreevat

ISEAS

Institute of Southeast Asian Studies, Singapore

First published in Singapore in 2006 by
Institute of Southeast Asian Studies
30 Heng Mui Keng Terrace
Pasir Panjang
Singapore 119614

Internet e-mail: publish@iseas.edu.sg
World Wide Web: http://bookshop.iseas.edu.sg

*The responsibility for facts and opinions in this publication rests exclusively
with the editor and contributors and their interpretations do not necessarily reflect
the views or the policy of the Institute or its supporters.*

ISEAS Library Cataloguing-in-Publication Data

Corporate governance in Thailand / edited by Sakulrat Montreevat.
1. Corporate governance—Thailand.
I.   Sakulrat Montreevat.
HD2741 C826   2006

ISBN 981-230-330-8 (soft cover)
ISBN 981-230-331-6 (hard cover)

Typeset by International Typesetters Pte. Ltd.
Printed in Singapore by Seng Lee Press Pte. Ltd.

Contents

List of Tables

List of Figures

Abbreviations

TAAT	Airports Authority of Thailand
AOT	Airports of Thailand Public Company Limited
BAY	Bank of Ayudhya Public Company Limited
BBL	Bangkok Bank Public Company Limited
BCP	Bangchak Petroleum Public Company Limited
BOT	Bank of Thailand
BPI	Bank of the Philippines Islands
CAHB	Commerce Asset-Holding Berhad
CAT	Communications Authority of Thailand
CEO	chief executive officer
CLSA	Credit Lyonnais Securities Asia Limited
Co. Ltd.	company limited
CU	Chulalongkorn University
EGCO	Electricity Generating Public Company Limited
EXIM	Export-Import Bank of Thailand
DTDB	DBS Thai Danu Bank Public Company Limited
FIDF	Financial Institutions Development Fund
FTI	Federation of Thai Industries
GHB	Government Housing Bank
HSBC	Hongkong and Shanghai Banking Corporation Limited

ICAAT	Institute of Certified Accountants and Auditors of Thailand
IFASB	Thailand Financial Accounting Standard Board
IGAAP	International Generally Accepted Accounting Principles
IIAT	Institute of Internal Auditors of Thailand
IOD	Thai Institute of Directors Association
KBANK	Kasikornbank Public Company Limited (former Thai Farmers Bank)
KTB	Krung Thai Bank Public Company Limited
MAI	Market for Alternative Investment
MOC	Ministry of Commerce
MOF	Ministry of Finance
NCGC	National Corporate Governance Committee
NIDA	National Institute of Development Administration
OECD	Organization of Economic Co-operation and Development
PCL	public company limited
PTT	Petroleum Authority of Thailand Public Company Limited
PTTEP	PTT Exploration and Production Public Company Limited
SCB	Siam Commercial Bank Public Company Limited
SEC	Securities and Exchange Commission
SET	Stock Exchange of Thailand
SMEs	small and medium enterprises
SME Bank	Small and Medium Enterprise Development Bank of Thailand
SOEs	state-owned enterprises
TFASB	Thailand Financial Accounting Standard Board
THAI	Thai Airways International Public Company Limited
TOT	Telephone Organization of Thailand
TRIS	Thai Rating and Information Services Company Limited
VAT	value added tax

Acknowledgements

This book is the result of the collaborative effort of six scholars and researchers who are experts in their field and who have generously carved out precious time to contribute to the volume. The editor of the volume is grateful to them for their input.

An earlier version of the chapters in this volume was first presented as papers at the Workshop on "Corporate Governance Practices and Challenges in Post-Crisis Thailand" held in Singapore in October 2003. The Workshop brought together Thai academics and practitioners in the field as well as academics and representatives from corporations in Singapore and Thailand to discuss issues related to corporate governance practices and challenges in post-crisis Thailand.

This volume has benefited from the insightful comments made by discussants and participants at the Workshop. The editor would like to thank the following people in particular, whose remarks, comments, and suggestions made at the Workshop have helped strengthen and enrich this book: Ms Kala Anandarajah of Rajah & Tann, Ms Patareeya Benjapolchai of the Stock Exchange of Thailand, Ms Janjaree Buranawej of Kasikornbank Public Company Limited, Mr Chalee Chantanayingyong of the Office of the Securities and Exchange Commission, Dr Sitanon Jesdapipat of Chulalongkorn University, Dr Ananchai Kongchan of

Chulalongkorn University, Dr Pallapa Ruangrong of Ministry of Finance, and Mr Sorayuth Vathanavisuth of Kay Lines Limited.

The editor would also like to express her gratitude to the staff at the Institute of Southeast Asian Studies for their tireless effort in attending to the minutiae of organizing the Workshop and for preparing this volume for publication.

Sakulrat Montreevat
May 2005

Contributors

Saowaluk CHEEVASITTIYANON is Senior Researcher at the Thailand Development Research Institute (TDRI) in Bangkok. She obtained her Masters degree in Economics from the University of Essex in the United Kingdom. Her research covers the regulation of stated-owned enterprises and competition policy. She is a co-author of *Improving Incentive System and Compensation System of State-Owned Enterprises* (2002).

Boonchai HONGCHARU is Associate Dean, Academic Affairs at the Graduate School of Business Administration, National Institute of Development Administration (NIDA) in Bangkok. Prior to joining NIDA, he was Product Development Manager at Shinawatra Computer and Communications Public Company Limited and Investment Analyst at Merrill Lynch (then Smith New Court) and Deutsche Morgan Grenfell. He received his Ph.D. from S.I. Newhouse School of Public Communications, Syracuse University. His research interests include corporate governance and marketing. He was a member of the Institute of Directors of East Asia Network and Peer Assistance Review Group (PARNET) of the Pacific Economic Cooperation Council (PECC) on corporate governance.

Sakulrat MONTREEVAT is a Fellow in the Regional Economic Studies programme at the Institute of Southeast Asian Studies (ISEAS) in Singapore. She holds a doctorate degree in Economics from the University of Hawaii at Manoa. She was formerly Chief of Macroeconomics at the Siam Commercial Bank Research Institute (SCBRI) and its Vice-President from 1997 to 1999. She also acted as Managing Editor of the SCBRI's economic journals over the same period. At ISEAS she has been Co-editor of the *ASEAN Economic Bulletin* since 2000. Her main research interests are financial crises and financial reforms in East Asia, and macroeconomic management in Thailand. Her research articles have been published in *Thammasat Economic Journal, AsiaInt Economic Intelligence, Asia Pacific Journal of Economics and Business*, and various ISEAS publications.

Bhanupong NIDHIPRABHA is Associate Professor in Economics at Thammasat University. He obtained his BA in Economics from Thammasat University, and his M.Sc. from the London School of Economics, after which he joined Thammasat University in 1977. He also has a Ph.D. in Economics from the Johns Hopkins University. His research interests are in the field of macroeconomics and international trade. His recently published articles include "Contractionary Devaluation Revisited: Can Appreciation Be Expansionary?" in *State, Market, Society and Economic Cooperation in Asia* (2004); "SPS and Thailand's Exports of Processed Food" in *Food Safety Regulation Concerns: The Developing Country Perspective* (2005); and "Implication of a Flexible Exchange Rate" in *Thailand Beyond the Crisis* (2005).

Deunden NIKOMBORIRAK is Research Director at the Thailand Development Research Institute, an independent economic policy think-tank in Bangkok. She obtained her doctorate degree in Economics from McGill University in Montreal, Canada. She has experience working in the area of competition law and policy, regulation, and privatization of public utilities and corporate governance, which included working on projects to build good corporate governance commissioned by the United Nations Development Program, transport pricing and subsidy commissioned by the National Economic and Social Development

Board, and a survey of market structure and practices in selected industries commissioned by the Ministry of Commerce of Thailand. She is currently Chairperson of the Commission on Competition for the ICC (International Chamber of Commerce) Thailand Executive Board. She also serves as adviser to the Subcommittee Monitoring Bilateral Free Trade Agreements between Thailand and Foreign Countries, House of Commons.

Saravuth PITIYASAK, Law Lecturer at the School of Law, Sukhothai Thammathirat Open University in Bangkok, received his Ph.D. in Legal Science (SJD) from the University of Hong Kong and his Master of Law from the University of Sydney. Some of his published articles include "Taxing E-Commerce in Thailand" in *Tax International Planning* (2002), "Thailand Debates Software Patents" in *Managing Intellectual Property* (2002), "Thai Electronic Transaction Act 2001: Recent Developments Surrounding IT Law in Thailand" in *World Internet Law Report* (2002), "Does Thai Law Provide Adequate Protection for Copyright Infringement on the Internet?" in *European Intellectual Property Review* (2003), "Electronic Contracts: Contract Law of Thailand, England and UNCITRAL Compared" in *Computers and Telecommunications Law Review* (2003), and "Recent Developments Surrounding Good Corporate Governance of Listed Companies in Thailand" in *Corporate Governance Compliance* (2004).

Introduction

Sakulrat Montreevat

1. Objectives

In recent years there has been considerable interest in finding out whether good corporate governance is practised in Southeast Asia. Indeed, this area of research has been particularly important in the light of the 1997 financial crisis and the resultant slowdown in investment in the post-crisis period. Clearly, both events have served as a wake-up call for Southeast Asian economies, and forced policy-makers in the region to place more emphasis on capital market development as well as to improve corporate governance practices in the business sector.

Generally, corporate governance structures in Southeast Asia share similar characteristics such as a high ownership concentration, bank-centric financial systems, ineffective shareholders' rights, and a low degree of transparency. In the pre-crisis period, the Thai economy relied heavily on bank lending as a source of funds. A majority of well-regarded analyses in the literature point out that what contributed to the depth of the 1997 financial crisis as well as the protracted period the Thai economy languished in the trough was the absence of a varied range of financing options as well as the poor corporate governance of Thai firms. Thailand then moved quickly to begin to develop its capital market.

The outcome of this is that the reliance of firms on bank loans as their main source of funds has since been gradually diluted by the ongoing measures to develop the Thai capital market. In addition, the concept of corporate governance is being widely promoted; guidelines as to what constitutes good corporate governance are articulated and measures implemented to encourage and increase compliance. These bold initial steps have triggered an evolutionary process of further improvement and fine-tuning in Thailand's corporate sector.

Based on such a background, this book explores how corporate governance is practised in four categories of corporate firms in Thailand: listed non-financial companies, commercial banks, state-owned enterprises, and unlisted companies. Its main objective is to shed light on the challenges confronting good corporate governance practices in each category of firms, as well as to provide some key policy recommendations to further raise the level of corporate governance already achieved.

2. Defining "Corporate Governance" in Thailand

Corporate governance is a business term that refers to a system of promoting fairness, transparency, and accountability in a company's conduct and principles. The concept of corporate governance varies widely among countries. In the United States and the United Kingdom, a firm is said to be practising "corporate governance" if the objective of its policy is to pursue the interests of its shareholders. In Japan, Germany, and France, however, the firm's objective is to function in the interests of a wider set of stakeholders, which includes employees and customers as well as shareholders (Allen and Gale 2002).

In Thailand, the term "corporate governance" has only become widely used after the 1997 crisis. *Ban Sart Phi Barn* and *Karn Kkum Kub Doo Lae Kij Ja Karn* are both the Thai equivalent of "corporate governance". The former term is more difficult to understand and so it is not widely used. The latter, which means "supervision" in direct translation, is easier to understand.

In fact, the Stock Exchange of Thailand (SET) started to promote the concept of corporate governance when it laid down the role of an audit committee in the SET in 1995. In 1996 the SET commissioned Price Waterhouse Management Consultants Limited to conduct the first corporate governance survey. At that time, "corporate governance" was defined as

> the system or process by which organizations are directed and controlled by the directors and senior management for the benefit of its stakeholders — shareholders, employees, customers, bankers and suppliers. (Price Waterhouse Management Consultants Limited 1977, p. II)

After the Working Group of Corporate Governance[1] was set up in 1999, corporate governance was used to refer to the managerial or internal procedures that enable a company to achieve its goals, which in principle should be to maximize long-term value for its shareholders (SEC 1999).

In 2001 the Committee on Corporate Governance Development set up by the SET proposed a broader concept of corporate governance:

> A set of structure and process of relationships between a company's management, its board and its shareholders to enhance its competitiveness towards business prosperity and long-term shareholder value by taking into consideration the interests of other stakeholders. (SET 2001, p. 4)

In reality, no single universal definition of "corporate governance" applies to all Thai companies. The Siam Cement Public Company Limited[2] has long operated its business in line with corporate governance for over the past two decades, its philosophy being:

> [T]he company should demonstrate a keen sense of responsibility towards the best interests of its shareholders, and that the company should, at the same time, be acutely aware of all environmental considerations and of the well-being of society and the nation as a whole. (http://www.cementhai. co.th/eng/about/about_corporate.html)

The company has one of the best public images of corporate ethics in Thai society.

The Electricity Generating Public Company Limited (EGCO)[3] conducts its business under the supervision of the board of directors with full accountability to shareholders and other stakeholders, as well as a commitment towards the environment, community, and country. The company belief has become practice since its incorporation in 1992 (EGCO 2002).

The Kasikornbank Public Company Limited[4] has applied the

"Statement of Corporate Principles", which includes the characteristics of good corporate governance, namely: integrity, transparency, independence, accountability, responsibility, fairness, social responsibility (http://www.kasikornbank.com/GlobalHome/EN/homepage.html). The bank has gained recognition for good corporate governance both from within Thailand as well as internationally.

According to the National Corporate Governance Committee (NCGC),[5] there are several ways of looking at corporate governance:

- as the relationship between the board of directors of a company, its management team, its shareholders and other stakeholders, which directs the company and monitors its operations;
- as the structure and internal processes of a corporate entity to ensure that the board of directors evaluate the performance of the management team transparently and effectively;
- as a system having the structure and processes of leadership and corporate control to establish a transparent working environment and to enhance the company's competitiveness by preserving capital and increasing long-term value for shareholders, taking into consideration business ethics, as well as the interests of other stakeholders and society.

(http://www.cgthailand.org/SetCG/about/about.html)

The establishment of the NCGC indicates that the issue of corporate governance has become a national agenda. In the initial stages, the emphasis of the NCGC lay mainly in the implementation of corporate governance in the Thai capital market, that is, listed companies, commercial banks, finance companies, and insurance companies. In the later stages, the scope of implementation also included other (private and state) enterprises outside the capital market (SEC 2002).

3. Composition of This Book

This edited volume consists of four chapters dealing with corporate governance issues in listed non-financial companies, commercial banks, state-owned enterprises, and unlisted companies.

In Chapter 1, Hongcharu reviews the development of corporate governance in Thailand and identifies the significant players promoting corporate governance in the Thai economy. Voluntary and regulatory approaches towards the development of successful corporate governance are also looked into, along with policy recommendations for consideration. The scope of the study covers listed non-financial companies. Two actual cases representing the worst and the best of corporate governance practices in post-crisis Thailand are illustrated in the chapter.

In Chapter 2, Nidhiprabha focuses on key issues in banking governance in the post-1997 financial crisis. He describes how corporate governance is practised among the top 25 Asian banks in terms of good governance, and investigates the relationship between good governance and the stock performance of Thai banks. The chapter also goes some way towards identifying challenges and possible additional policies that can further enhance good corporate governance in the Thai banking system.

In Chapter 3, Nikomborirak and Cheevasittiyanon discuss governance issues of state-owned enterprises (SOEs), including the composition of the board of directors, qualifications of the CEO, the level of transparency in management, accountability of executives, equality between the government and private shareholders in a partially privatized enterprise, as well as the trade practices of SOEs. The authors finally provided some recommendations on how the governance of SOEs can be improved.

In Chapter 4, Pitiyasak reviews two Thai company laws — Public Limited Companies Act and Civil and Commercial Code. His analysis focuses on mechanisms for strengthening good corporate governance in Thai companies. Towards the end of the chapter, he provides some recommendations for promoting greater corporate governance in unlisted companies.

This book is probably the first of an in-depth examination of how companies both inside and outside the Thai capital market put corporate governance into practice and the challenges they face. Readers will agree that better and more useful approaches and measures should be considered for adoption. In addition, the public should be reminded about the importance of good corporate governance.

NOTES

1. The Working Group set up by the Securities and Exchange Commission (SEC) constitutes representatives from the Ministry of Finance (MOF), the Ministry of Commerce (MOC), the Stock Exchange of Thailand (SET), the Institute of Certified Accountants and Auditors of Thailand (ICAAT), the Institute of Internal Auditors of Thailand (IIAT), as well as the SEC itself.

2. The Siam Cement Public Company Limited was founded in 1913 by King Rama VI. At present, its businesses are mainly in paper and packaging, petrochemicals, cement, building products, ceramics, and distribution, which include international trading, and two more businesses of properties and holding companies.

3. The Electricity Generating Public Company Limited (EGCO) is the first Independent Power Producer in Thailand through the partial privatization of state enterprises.

4. The Kasikornbank Public Company Limited was established in 1945. The Bank is the third largest commercial bank in Thailand as measured by total assets, loans, and deposits.

5. The National Corporate Governance Committee (NCGC) was established in 2002 for the purpose of setting up policies, measures, and schemes to upgrade the level of corporate governance in Thai business. The NCGC consists of the following members: the prime minister or the assigned deputy prime ministers, minister for finance, minister for commerce, permanent-secretary of the minister for finance, permanent-secretary of the minister for commerce, governor of the Bank of Thailand (BOT), secretary-general of the Office of the Securities and Exchange Commission (SEC), president of the Stock Exchange of Thailand (SET), president of Thai Chamber of Commerce (TCC), president of the Federation of Thai Industries (FTI), president of Thai Bankers' Association, president of the Certified Accountants and Auditors of Thailand, president of the Listed Companies Association, president of the Association of Securities Companies, president of the Association of Investment Management Companies (AIMC), president of the Thai Investors' Association, president of the Thai Institute of Directors' Association, and assistant secretary-general of the SEC.

REFERENCES

Alba, Pedro, Stijn Claessens, and Simeon Djankov. "Thailand's Corporate Financing and Governance Structures: Impact on Firms' Competitiveness". Paper presented at the conference on "Thailand's Dynamic Economic Recovery and Competitiveness", organized by the World Bank at Bangkok, 20–21 May 1998.

Allen, Franklin, and Douglas Gale. "A Comparative Theory of Corporate Governance".

http://fic.wharton.upenn.edu/fic/papers/03/p0327.html (accessed 22 December 2002).

Asian Development Bank (ADB). *Corporate Governance and Finance in East Asia: A Study of Indonesia, Republic of Korea, Malaysia, Philippines, and Thailand.* Vol. I: A Consolidated Report. Manila: Asian Development Bank, 2000.

Electricity Generating Public Company Limited (EGCO). *Annual Report 2001.* Bangkok: Pink Blue Black & Orange, 2002.

Price Waterhouse Management Consultant Limited. *Corporate Governance in Thailand: A Price Waterhouse Survey.* Commissioned by the Stock Exchange of Thailand. Bangkok: Price Waterhouse Management Consultants, January 1997.

Securities and Exchange Commission (SEC). "Report on Enhancing Good Corporate Governance of Thai Listed Companies". Mimeographed. April 1999.

―――. *First Decade of the Thai SEC and Capital Market in Thailand (1992–2002).* Bangkok: Office of the Securities and Exchange Commission, 2002.

Stock Exchange of Thailand (SET). *Report on Corporate Governance.* Bangkok: SET, August 2001.

http://www.cgthailand.org/SetCG/about/about.html.

http://www.cementhai.co.th/eng/about/about_corporate.html.

http://www.kasikornbank.com/GlobalHome/EN/homepage.html.

1

Transparency and Accountability of Listed Non-Financial Companies in Post-Crisis Thailand

Boonchai Hongcharu

Transparency in reporting information to the public and accountability to the public for its activities are very important for good corporate governance. After the Asian financial crisis in mid-1997, there was much discussion and numerous activities launched to improve corporate governance in Thailand, especially for companies listed on the Stock Exchange of Thailand (SET). This chapter reviews the development of corporate governance in Thailand and identifies the significant players involved in promoting corporate governance. It also looks at voluntary and regulatory approaches towards good corporate governance, along with possible policy recommendations. However, the scope of this study covers the listed non-financial companies only. Two actual cases representing the worst and best of corporate governance practices in post-crisis Thailand are also provided.

1. The Development of Corporate Governance

Even before the financial crisis of 1997, some firms in Thailand were already practising varying degrees of corporate governance. For instance, Siam Cement Public Company Limited, the largest building and construction conglomerate, adopted the code of best practices that IBM Thailand Company Limited adhered to. In 1996 the SET commissioned Price Waterhouse Management Consultants Limited to conduct the first survey to find out how Thai companies fared with regard to corporate governance. The data gathered from the survey would then be used to help Thailand develop its capital market.

An analysis of the financial crisis in July 1997 reveals that structural weaknesses in the Thai economy had allowed massive capital inflows into the economy. The problem was worsened by the lack of proper macroeconomic management mechanisms, coupled with bad corporate governance among companies that do not observe the separation of management and control. Moreover, reckless lending was prevalent at the time and loan growth was almost the only factor that financial institutions focused on. It was therefore not surprising that most corporations invested heavily using the foreign capital inflows that passed through the local financial institutions. At the same time, there was a lack of accountability and transparency in the expropriation of funds.

Before the financial crisis, the concept of corporate governance was not widely known among the general public; even the significant players, such as management, shareholders, and stakeholders, were not aware of the term. There was no translation of the term in Thai at that time. Soon, however, with the concerted effort of major institutions in the public and private sectors, the public has been gradually educated about corporate governance and its importance to the Thai economy. This chapter reviews the roles played by the major institutions and organizations in their effort to promote good corporate governance in Thailand. The chapter ends with several policy recommendations to build on the groundwork already put in place and to spread the culture of good corporate governance.

2. Significant Players Involved in Promoting Good Corporate Governance

2.1 Government

The Asian financial crisis came as a shock to everyone, and the imperative to institutionalize good corporate governance became obvious. Soon after this rude awakening, corporate governance became the central topic when the APEC Finance Ministers met in Kananaskis, Canada, in May 1998. Then, at the Symposium on Corporate Governance in APEC: Rebuilding Asian Growth held in Sydney, Australia, held on 1–3 November 1998, directions were set to promote corporate governance so that each government would play an active role in its own reform strategy (Australian APEC Study Centre 1998).

Since the financial crisis, the Thai government has passed numerous laws, one of which is the Accounting Act, and implemented several measures to promote good corporate governance. Also being implemented are various legal instruments such as the Public Limited Company Act, the Securities and Exchange Commission Act, the Bank of Thailand Act, and the bankruptcy laws.

Other measures include the Thaksin administration's establishment of the National Corporate Governance Committee (NCGC), whose purpose is to support and promote good corporate governance on a national basis. The government also designated 2002 as the year for the inauguration of corporate governance campaigns.

Corporate governance has thus become a national agenda, and it involves the following:

- a gradual but continuous implementation of the concept;
- the focus being placed on the benefits of corporate governance rather than its legal enforcement;
- impositioning of stiff punishment for violators;
- use of both incentives and punishment to promote its practice;
- drafting of new laws with practical considerations;
- active public relations campaigns.

(http://www.sec.or.th/goodgov/index.shtml, 2003)

2.2 Supporting Agencies

Supporting agencies are independent agencies that help in the implementation of the government's policy to promote good corporate governance. These include the Securities and Exchange Commission (SEC), the Stock Exchange of Thailand (SET), the Thai Institute of Directors Association (IOD), and Thai Rating and Information Services Company Limited (TRIS).

The SEC is responsible for the legal and regulatory aspects of corporate governance, while the SET promotes voluntary approaches towards corporate governance. For example, the SET requires listed companies to elect independent directors, set up an audit committee, and recommend that they form a remuneration committee, which most of the listed companies have voluntarily complied with.

When the SET targeted 2003 — "SET Vision 2003" — as the year to reach "International Standards of Enforcement and Corporate Governance" (SET June 2000), it regularly reported on the progress made towards achieving its objectives. The SET has initiated the creation of education programmes to train various groups of people dealing with listed firms, for example, investors, directors, management, and securities firms. Since August 2003 the SET has put together five courses of the Director Accreditation Program for directors of listed companies to learn what are their basic roles and responsibilities. It also supports the training provided by the IOD by funding 75 per cent of the training fee that the company pays for their directors' training.

Under the new laws, the roles of the SET, SEC, and Ministry of Commerce (MOC) are more clearly defined. The SET is the forefront regulator responsible for monitoring listed companies to ensure their compliance with the Securities and Exchange Act and Public Limited Company Act along with other SEC and SET rules. If a listed company is suspected of having violated any of the laws and regulations, however, the SET's task is to undertake the preliminary investigation.

The SEC monitors the performance of auditors of listed companies and securities firms to ensure that they comply with the laws and regulations. It will also undertake an in-depth investigation for cases referred by the SET. While the SEC covers listed companies only, the MOC monitors the compliance of all public companies.

The IOD was founded in 1999 with the support of the BOT, the SET, the Capital Market Development Fund Foundation, and the World Bank. The IOD is an independent training centre that develops training programmes for directors and executives in Thailand. Its core programme, the Directors Certification Program (DCP), was developed under the supervision of the Australian Institute of Company Directors (AICD). The scope of the DCP includes director knowledge (the practice of directorship and company law), financial knowledge (introduction to financial statements and assessing company performance), strategy knowledge (strategic direction, strategic human resources, and board effectiveness improvement), and business knowledge (trade practices, risk assessment, and contract law). The IOD launched its first DCP training in July 2000, followed by a one-day programme designed specially to equip chairpersons with the required knowledge, called "Chairman 2000" in November 2000 (Thai Institute of Directors Association 2000).

The TRIS was founded in 1993 with the support of the Ministry of Finance (MOF) and the BOT for credit rating purposes. In 1995 the company launched its performance evaluation services. By 2002 it began to undertake corporate governance rating, using the methodology adopted by models worldwide. It has been selected by the SEC to rate how firms listed on the SET fare in terms of corporate governance. Currently, firms are not required to subject themselves to the corporate governance rating, though they are encouraged to do so. Some of the benefits of a good rating by the SEC include being eligible for the fast-track process for the public offerings of securities and a 50 per cent reduction of its offering fee and the annual fee. The SET also offers a 50 per cent discount of the annual fee for listed companies that have attained a good corporate governance rating. Since the inception of corporate governance rating in 2002, TRIS has rated four listed companies.

2.3 Companies

2.3.1 Non-Financial Companies

Listed non-financial companies are increasingly seeking to improve their corporate governance practices. Besides following the best practices of the SET, some companies are promoting themselves as a supporter of good corporate governance. For instance, Siam Cement

Public Company Limited, Thailand's largest building and construction material conglomerate, advertised on television and other media that it has embraced good corporate governance and brought the term to the public. Other companies include Electricity Generating Public Company Limited, one of the corporate governance award winners, and Thai Union Frozen Products Public Company Limited. Among the non-listed firms, most of the former state enterprises have also improved and promoted transparency and corporate governance through advertising, for example, the TOT Public Company Limited, Thailand's largest telephone operators.

2.3.2 Financial Companies

Financial institutions are also significant players, as they are both creditors and debtors of most firms in Thailand. A large number of banks and finance companies were reckless in their lending during the financial crisis. This has prompted most financial institutions to assess the corporate governance risks of the companies that want to borrow money from them. So, financial institutions have become more prudent in their lending since. Through the Bank of Thailand Act, the Commercial Banking Act, and the Act on the Undertaking of Finance Business, Securities Business, and Credit Foncier Business, banks and finance companies are required to be more circumspect in their lending decisions. Most financial institutions have put pressure on the companies they lend money to, and this has forced them to comply with good corporate governance practice.

2.4 Investors

Thailand has an increasing number of institutional investors — for example, mutual fund companies, government pension funds. Traditionally, institutional investors do not have sufficient bargaining power vis-à-vis the listed companies, as it is generally the major shareholders who control the agenda of the shareholders meeting and management decisions. Another reality is that even if institutional investors have large funds to invest, they may not want to be directly involved in the management of the company. Nevertheless, institutional investors can indirectly improve the standards of good corporate governance. As significant players in the securities market, institutional investors should make it a point to attend shareholders meetings to represent minority investors who are their customers. Along with the SEC or the SET, institutional investors can help investigate insider trading and other improper or bad corporate governance practices among listed companies and lodge a report to the relevant agencies.

Minority shareholders or individual investors have often been the losers because listed companies are often found wanting in the area of corporate governance. They have been victims to these companies and are bearing heavy losses from their investments on the stock exchange when the SET index plunged from a peak of 1,700 points in 1993 to 200 points in 1998 before gradually rising to 500 to 600 points in 2003. It has been found that most of the minority investors are punters who do not have sufficient knowledge about investment in the stock market and who also fail to exercise their rights as shareholders.

It is suggested that the SET, the Asset Management Association, the Securities Brokerage Association, educational institutions or universities, and the Association of Individual Investors collaborate to advise individual investors about investing in the stock market and teach them how to assess whether any company listed on the SET do in fact practise good corporate governance.

2.5 Stakeholders

A company's stakeholders include all parties involved with the company, for example, customers, suppliers, employees, regulators, neighbouring communities. Stakeholders form one of the important groups that can help promote corporate governance. However, they are often ignored by the supporting agencies or the government as stakeholders are made up of many parties, and have to be constantly reminded about the importance of good corporate governance. Nevertheless, as companies increasingly come to value their stakeholders, they tend to do what is right to retain their continuous support. With the rising sense of the importance of corporate social responsibility today, some companies have launched campaigns to improve the quality of life of their neighbouring communities, educate the public about the notion of corporate governance, clean up the environment, and so forth. The corporate advertisements of many listed companies also express their concern for these issues. Some of such companies are Advanced Info Service Public Company Limited, Total Access Communication Public Company Limited (listed in Singapore), a subsidiary of United Communication Industry Public Company Limited, Bangchak Petroleum Public Company Limited, Thai Airways International Public Company Limited, National Fertilizer Public Company Limited, and Saha Patanapibul Public Company Limited, a consumer goods conglomerate.

2.6 Professional Associations

Professional associations have been a significant factor helping to raise the level of corporate governance in the respective professions and in related industries, especially in the accounting profession. The Accounting Act, which is consistent with the International Accounting Standards (IAS), was passed and had been enacted with the support of the Thai government and the SET. To monitor and control the best practices of accounting and auditing in Thailand, the Institute of Certified Accountants and Auditors of Thailand (ICAAT), an independent self-regulated professional entity, was set up. In addition, the Thailand Financial Accounting Standard Board (TFASB) was established specifically for the purpose of setting the accounting standards.

Moreover, the role of professional associations in promoting corporate governance should be extended into other industries as well and not merely be restricted to the professions directly involved in corporate governance issues. In this way the concept of corporate governance can permeate into wider fields of the professions.

2.7 Academic Institutions

In fact, universities should play an active role in developing good corporate governance. The involvement of academic institutions in promoting corporate governance, however, is still limited.

The National Institute of Development Administration (NIDA), a government-owned graduate university, is actively involved in projects on corporate governance and corporate social responsibility. Chulalongkorn University (CU) and the World Bank (WB) have initiated a joint project called CU-WB Knowledge Management Project, which serves as a repository for all World Bank project documents.

3. Approaches towards Good Corporate Governance in Post-Crisis Thailand

After the financial crisis in 1997, the lack of corporate governance has often been cited as one of the major factors leading to the demise of corporations. The collapse of a number of banks and finance companies in Thailand was the main factor that led to a search for the root cause of the crisis. Even though financial institutions were blamed for reckless lending, the lack of transparency and accountability among non-financial companies clearly reveals the problems on the borrowers' side.

This pushed the government and supporting agencies to be decisive about strengthening corporate governance among listed firms through a series of education programmes on best practices initiated by the SET, and the strict enforcement of the SEC. The four elements that are used by the SET and SEC as rationale for promoting good corporate governance are similar to those set by the OECD — *OECD Principles of Corporate Governance* (OECD 1999). These are:

- Fairness: Outside shareholders and creditors should be protected and treated fairly by the inside shareholders against fraud and misconduct.
- Transparency: The company should disclose accurate and timely information about the status of its financial and non-financial details to the public in its annual report. It should also state whether it is adopting the International Accounting Standards (IAS).
- Accountability: The company should set up a system with clearly defined responsibilities for the board of directors and the executives who are to be accountable to shareholders and creditors.
- Responsibility: The company should have responsibilities to shareholders and stakeholders, including employees, consumers, suppliers, creditors, government, neighbouring communities, and so forth. As a corporate citizen, the company has responsibilities to pay taxes and protect the environment, health, and safety of all stakeholders and the communities.

The measures used to entrench corporate governance in business in Thailand can be classified under two categories: voluntary and regulatory approaches:

3.1 Voluntary Approach
towards Good Corporate Governance

The voluntary approach gives companies the freedom to implement what the authorities have suggested for improving their corporate governance practices without mandatory enforcement. Rewards or contests are normally provided as an incentive for companies that choose to comply with or put into practice as best as they can good corporate governance practices. It has been noted that some of the measures under the voluntary category have over a period of time moved over to the mandatory category.

Some measures under the voluntary category include the following:

3.1.1 Board Composition

The SET had initiated several measures to promote good corporate governance through encouraging listed companies to voluntarily comply with its code of best practices. These initiatives have now become requirements on the board composition of listed firms.

- Independent directors: The SET requires all listed firms to elect at least two independent directors who do not hold any position in the management and are not employees of the company. They must not be an executive director or an authorized director of the company. The independent directors should represent the interests of minority shareholders and express useful and reliable opinions on behalf of the shareholders to the board. The target is to increase the number of independent directors on the board to one-third (33 per cent) of the total number of board members.

- The audit committee: In early 1998 the SET suggested that listed companies form an audit committee, and even provided an incentive of 15 per cent discount of the annual fee, if the firm implementated it. At present, all listed firms are required to have at least three independent directors serving as audit committee members. Members of the audit committee are expected to be impartial and be able to express their views independently. According to the SET, the major duties of an audit committee member include overseeing the listed company's financial reporting process and the disclosure of all financial information, setting up adequate and effective internal control and internal audit systems, preventing activities that would cause a conflict of interests, and ensuring that a listed company complies with relevant laws and regulations.

3.1.2 Guidelines and Best Practices

From 1997 to 2001, the SET issued guidelines and best practices as follows:

- November 1997: The Code of Best Practices for Directors of Listed Companies (SET October 1999) aimed at setting ethical and corporate governance standards for all board members and strengthening the confidence of shareholders, investors, and other stakeholders after the financial crisis;
- January 1998: The Roles, Duties, and Responsibilities of the Directors of Listed Companies (SET October 1998);
- October 1998: Guidelines on Internal Audit;
- July 1999: Best Practice Guidelines for the Audit Committee (SET October 1999). These best practice guidelines are constantly revised and updated;
- January 2000: *Report on Corporate Governance* (updated version published in March 2001 and August 2001).

All these guidelines and best practices constitute voluntary approaches that the SET has laid down for listed companies to work towards. Some of the guidelines and best practices have since turned into listing requirements, for example, the number of independent directors and the formation of an audit committee for listed firms.

Moreover, the SET initially encouraged and later made it a requirement that all listed companies state in their annual reports whether they have complied with the code of best practices and provide their rationale in the case of non-compliance. This information will be publicized for investors to evaluate the company's management. It is one of the several measures to increase information disclosure and transparency of listed firms.

3.1.3 Disclosure

To promote greater transparency and good corporate governance, the SET has set disclosure-based criteria for new listings, focusing on reliable, accurate, and complete information about the financial and non-financial performance of a company. Listed companies are encouraged to disclose as much information to the public as possible.

Besides the information disclosure criteria set up by the SET, the new Accounting Act requires accurate financial information disclosure in accordance with the International Accounting Standards (IAS). With this new accounting law passed in mid-2000, the accounting and auditing standards in Thailand will be more transparent and in line with international best practices. The SET will not accept financial statements that do not comply with the Thai General Acceptable Accounting Principles (GAAP). Furthermore, the SET has formed a Committee on Financial Disclosure comprising accounting professionals and experts to consider the accuracy and transparency of financial information of listed companies.

Furthermore, as of January 1998, every listed company needs to set up an internal control and audit system to monitor its financial information and provide reliable accounting and financial information to the public in a timely manner.

3.1.4 Protection of Shareholders' Rights

The SET tries very hard to encourage minority shareholders to monitor the performance of listed companies. This includes initiating legal requirements for proxy solicitations to ensure that a written proxy contains sufficient information for shareholders to act upon, for example, the number of shares held and entitlement to vote, details on the issues to be voted on, and the number of votes for approval or disapproval. These procedures for voting by proxy and other necessary documents have already been included in the Public Limited Company Act.

Cumulative voting is another mechanism that minority shareholders can use to exercise their rights to appoint or dismiss the director of a listed company. However, minority shareholders must form an organization to monitor the performance of the listed companies. In this regard, the Association of Individual Investors was set up in May 2002 and has bought shares in listed companies so that the association, on behalf of the minority shareholders, can actively participate in annual shareholders' meetings (ww.sec.or.th/goodgov/progress.shtml, 2003).

With regard to institutional investors, the Association of Institutional Investors, under the Government Pension Fund's leadership, has formed an association to monitor the corporate governance practices of listed companies and to protect shareholders' rights (www.sec.or.th/goodgov/progress.shtml, 2003).

As for majority shareholders, the SET has drafted the Best Practice of Majority Shareholders and distributed the document in March 2003. This best practice guidelines will highlight the suggested roles and responsibilities of major shareholders including government policy on shareholding in listed companies (www.sec.or.th/goodgov/progress.shtml, 2003).

3.1.5 Educating Good Corporate Governance

The SET has arranged for numerous seminars and events to disseminate the necessary information and knowledge on good corporate governance to listed companies, related agencies, and the general public.

Informative documents that the SET had distributed to listed companies during 2002–2003 included:

- 15 Principles of Good Corporate Governance;
- Checklist of SET's 15 Corporate Governance Principles for listed companies to assess themselves (January 2003);
- examples of board self-assessment (December 2002);
- the 2001 Directors' Compensation (December 2002);
- examples on how to report the implementation of the 15 Principles (December 2002);
- Best Practices of Shareholders (March 2003);
- Risk-Management Guidelines (August 2003).

For more information, go to: www.set.or.th/isc/infoserv/download_p1.html#governance.

Moreover, the SET has arranged for various seminars for listed companies in 2003. They are:

- How to report the implementation of 15 corporate governance principles in the annual report and annual registration form;
- Risk-management guidelines for directors;
- Risk-management guidelines for executives;
- Directors' roundtable sessions.

Besides the SET, many professional associations also help to educate their members on corporate governance. These include:

- The Institute of Certified Accountants and Auditors of Thailand (ICAAT) has started training programmes for accountants to provide them with the same corporate governance standards. The Institute also plans to train chief financial officers (CFO) and chief accounting officers (CAO) for improving financial reports (www. sec.or.th/goodgov/progress.shtml, 2003).
- The Federation of Thai Industries (FTI), an association of representatives from various industries in Thailand, has drafted the Code of Ethics of Industrial Operators as a guideline of best practices for the management of Thai industries.
- The Thai Chamber of Commerce drafted the Code of Ethics for Directors and Officers and Principles of Corporate Governance for its members. It has plans to launch a Q-Mark programme to award members who practise good corporate governance (www.sec.or.th/ goodgov/progress.shtml, 2003).

3.1.6 Integrated Marketing Communication Campaigns

As the government plans to use active public relations campaign to promote corporate governance, integrated marketing communication to support the endeavours is needed. In August 2002 the government started disseminating information on corporate governance via various media, for example, television programmes (*Route to Corporate Governance and Economic Markets*), radio programmes (short features and talk shows), and print material (*Corporate Governance World* and articles in the *Journal of the Stock Exchange of Thailand*). The government also conducted a roadshow for foreign investors to increase their confidence and awareness of corporate governance in Thailand. The first roadshow trip was in January 2003. The training on corporate governance for the press was conducted at the end of 2002.

The National Corporate Governance Committee (NCGC) approved the logo and the slogan "Good corporate governance creates transparency, boosts confidence for all". On 10 April 2003 it launched a website www. cgthailand.org, which disseminates information on corporate governance (www.sec.or.th/goodgov/progres3.shtml, 2003).

3.1.7 Awards and Contests

The Thai government and the supporting agencies organize contests on corporate governance and award companies that rank best in terms of their corporate governance practices. Some of these contests include the Asia-Pacific Annual Conference and Best Practices on Corporate Governance Award Contest put together by the Institute of Internal Auditors of Thailand (IIAT), an affiliate of the US-based Institute of Internal Auditors. The Best Practice on Corporate Governance Award Contest was held to promote excellent achievements made in corporate governance and the audit committee of companies and state-owned enterprises operating in Thailand. The criteria for judgement are: (a) effectiveness and leadership of the board and board committee; and (b) principles applied to shareholders and stakeholders: disclosure process and related transparency in management practices.

The SET also held a contest to rate listed companies on various components. One of the awards was the Best Corporate Governance Report. The rating was based on the 15 corporate governance criteria set by the SET. There were 15 companies receiving the 2003 SET Awards on Best Corporate Governance Report: Aromatics (Thailand) Public Company Limited, Bangkok Aviation Fuel Services Public Company Limited, Banpu Public Company Limited, Electricity Generating Public Company Limited, Precious Shipping Public Company Limited, Siam Cement Public Company Limited, Ratchaburi Electricity Generating Holding Public Company Limited, PTT Exploration and Production Public Company Limited, Thai Pineapple Public Company Limited, Yuasa Battery (Thailand) Public Company Limited, Ayudhya Investment and Trust Public Company Limited, Kasikornbank Public Company Limited, Siam Commercial Bank Public Company Limited, Siam Industrial Credit Finance Public Company Limited, and Thai Insurance Public Company Limited.

The SEC also plans to announce the Disclosure Awards for 40 listed companies that comply with the disclosure rules of the SEC. There are about 130 listed companies participating in the programme, and the SEC is in the process of selecting the qualified companies.

The awards and contests are incentives for companies to improve their levels of corporate governance. Companies judged to be having good corporate governance serve as a benchmark for other companies to measure their progress against. It is hoped that the awards and contests will continue to be held.

3.1.8 Research and Monitoring Studies on Corporate Governance

Alba, Claessens, and Djankov have conducted a policy study on *Thailand's Corporate Financing and Governance Structures: Impact on Firms' Competitiveness* (1998) by reviewing the literature and using available financial statements of listed firms on the SET. The researchers found problems in five areas relating to corporate governance: concentration of ownership, a higher level of diversification, weak market incentives, little protection for minority shareholders, lack of accounting standards and practices.

Several parties have conducted corporate governance surveys to assess the level of corporate governance attained in Thailand:

- Corporate governance survey conducted by Price Waterhouse Management Consultants Ltd. in 1996;
- Corporate governance survey conducted by the SET in 1999;
- Survey on "Audit Committee: Problems and Trend" by the SET in 2000;
- Survey on "Director's Role, Duty and Compensation" by the IOD in 2002.

More of such research is needed to monitor the progress of corporate governance in Thailand.

3.1.9 Corporate Governance Rating

The SEC has appointed TRIS to rate the level of corporate governance practised in listed Thai companies. The rating is based on four criteria: shareholders' rights (20 per cent of total score), composition and roles of the board of directors and management (40 per cent of total score), information disclosure (25 per cent of total score), and corporate governance culture (15 per cent of total score). The ratings are subdivided thus: 7.0 to 10.0 (good to excellence), 5.0 to less than 7.0 (moderate), and less than 5.0 (improvement recommended). The SEC and SET provide incentives for listed companies that participate in the rating and that have attained a score of 7 and above. For companies with a score of 7 and above, the SEC grants them a fast-track process for any public offerings of securities and the company's offering fees and annual fees are reduced by 50 per cent. Moreover, the SET gives them a discount of 50 per cent for their annual fees for two years (www.tris. co.th/products_services/governance_eng.html, 2003).

3.2 Regulatory Approach and Legal Instruments

The regulatory approach involves legal enforcement to ensure good corporate governance practices. Generally, legal enforcement requires the drafting of new laws with penalty clauses for infringements. Some of the penalties set are based on years of experiments with the voluntary approach.

Since the financial crisis, Thailand has passed new laws or is in the process of drafting new laws to enhance corporate governance. The Accounting Act was passed; however, the Public Companies Act and Securities Exchange Act are making slow progress (World Bank 2003). Some of these laws deal with financial institutions and the Bank of Thailand, which are not being dealt with in this chapter. Only new laws that are concerned with non-financial listed companies are reviewed here.

3.2.1 The Accounting Act

With the establishment of Thailand Financial Accounting Standard Board (TFASB), an independent board that sets the accounting standards, the Thai government initiated the drafting of laws to set standards for the accounting profession. Working in partnership with this board, the ICAAT also functions as an independent professional institute to raise standards for the accounting profession.

A higher standard in accounting is regarded as one of the first steps to improve corporate structure in Thailand. It enhances transparency and good corporate governance through a close monitoring of accounting practices. Therefore, accounting standards that follow international best practices were introduced and adopted by the ICAAT during 1998–99.

3.2.2 The Securities and Exchange Act

The first amendment to the Securities and Exchange Act (SEA) requires that more than half of the number of directors of the SEC are to be full-time directors and the number of directors who previously held political appointments are to be reduced. At present, half of the directors are selected from the securities industry and the rest by the government. In addition, the finance minister is automatically appointed chairman of the SEC board. The amendment of the Securities and Exchange Act will grant autonomy to the SET and it can become a private company.

Some of the amendments concerning corporate governance are related to securities and securities exchange regulatory organization, disclosure of information before and after a securities offering, board of directors of the securities exchange, unfair securities trading practices (that is, insider trading, market manipulation, imparting or disseminating of information that may mislead investors), and proxy solicitation (www. sec.or.th/secen1/legal/secact/newact.shtml, 1998).

3.2.3 The Public Limited Company Act

Improvement in the protection of minority shareholders' rights will be included in this new draft. This will give them a chance to vote to dismiss the directors of the company. Investors will have more access to information related to the performance of the public company. The new version will improve the call for a shareholders meeting, the duties of directors, the roles and responsibilities of directors and executives, and penalties for fraudulent practices.

3.2.4 Other Reforms That Would Help the Regulatory Approach

Even though some of the important legal instruments have been passed, it is still uncertain if the enforcement would be successful. Thus, there should be further improvements to hasten the legal process so that due penalties are meted out in a timely way to those who violate securities laws. Similarly, timeliness should also apply when victims of a misconduct seek redress against the directors or the management who violated securities laws or engage in poor corporate governance practices.

3.2.5 Significant Issues Concerning the Legal Instruments

Even though more legal instruments are now available in Thailand to enhance corporate governance, there are also obstacles that inhibit successful enactment and prosecution. The lack of information necessary to prosecute those who violate corporate governance–related laws can lead to lengthy and sometimes unsuccessful prosecution. In general, the legal process in Thailand is lengthy. In the case of the Asia Trust Bank, which was one of the few cases in which the management team was taken to court because of poor corporate governance, it took a decade to finalize the case. Part of the reason for these long-drawn cases could be that the Eastern culture does not see legal instruments as a effective means to solve problems, and out-of-court settlement or negotiation seems to be preferred.

4. Costs and Benefits of Listed Non-Financial Companies that Implement Good Corporate Governance

It is obvious that the implementation of good corporate governance can be a burden to listed non-financial companies. The costs include expenditure incurred in disclosing its business activities and being transparent in the financial statements, setting up an internal control system, searching and hiring qualified auditors and directors, training of directors and employees, and being accountable to all stakeholders, and so forth. Moreover, these are not one-off costs; instead they are costs that have to be incurred on an ongoing basis. The question then is: What do listed non-financial firms get from practising good corporate governance?

It is encouraging to note that a research done by the IOD in 2002 indicates that there is a positive relationship between market-to-book value and corporate governance rating. This is depicted by the linear relationship between corporate governance rating and market-to-book

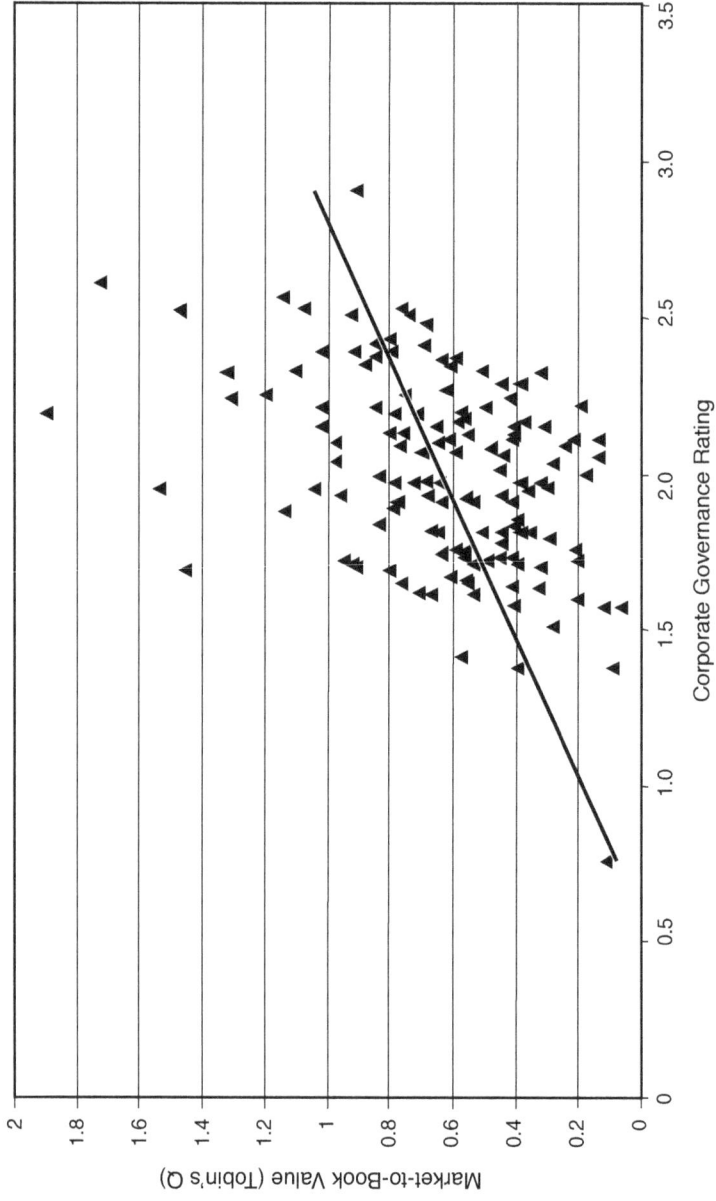

Figure 1.1
Correlation between Corporate Governance Rating and Market-to-Book Value

Source: Thai Institute of Directors Association (2002).

value in Figure 1.1. The relationship implies that good corporate governance rating is related to higher market capitalization, which, in turn, translates to higher shareholder wealth.

Furthermore, the correlation between the two factors looks likely to be exponential. If this can be confirmed, any increment in rating a company receives for good corporate governance would be translated into a rise in market-to-book value that is several times that much higher. This is an interesting observation for future research.

Although the relationship between corporate governance rating and the level of stock price requires further research, it is apparent that the benefits of good corporate governance outweigh the costs in the long run. Corporate governance ensures fair treatment for all stakeholders and investors are more likely to invest in companies that practise good corporate governance. Moreover, creditors are increasingly attaching a higher weightage to corporate governance when making decisions to extend loans to companies.

5. Worst and Best Cases of Corporate Governance Practices in Post-Crisis Thailand

To illustrate how Thai companies fare in terms of corporate governance in Thailand after the financial crisis, two actual companies representing the worst and the best of such cases are given below.

5.1 The Worst Case: Roynet Public Company Limited

Despite the efforts of various authorities and business participants in Thailand to strengthen good corporate governance, the most challenging case so far that would test whether all these efforts have been worthwhile happened in 2002. The company in question was the Roynet Public Company Limited.

Roynet was one of the Internet service providers that received concessions from the Communication Authority of Thailand in March 2000. Founded by Mr Kittipat Yaoprukse, Roynet had three main business units: Internet services (90 per cent of its 2002 income), computer training courses (1 per cent of its 2002 income), and other related services (9 per cent of its 2002 income), together with homepage construction, domain registration, hardware and software sales, and system development and implementation (www.roynet.co.th).

The company had a registered capital of 61 million baht and was listed on the Market for Alternative Investment (MAI), the second board of the SET on 25 October 2001.

In early 2003 the SEC found that Roynet had committed at least three offences:

- *Accounting Fraud:* Roynet had to restate its third quarter of 2002 financial results as it booked revenue in its financial statement although no actual sales occurred. The restatement of financial results came after Roynet's auditor issued an unqualified statement. Finally, the company announced that it in fact made a loss of 13.22 million baht, and that its earlier-reported profit of 11.87 million baht was incorrect.
- *Insider Trading:* The Yaoprukse family, who were the major shareholders of Roynet, had used internal financial information to enrich themselves. Aware that the earnings would be disastrous, the family sold their 60 per cent stake in 2002, earning approximately 50 million baht.
- *Disclosure of Information:* The sale of the Yaoprukse family violated two provisions of the Securities and Exchange Act. One provision states that the company management needs to disclose all changes in its shareholding to the public. The other is the disclosure of changes in shareholding of more than 5 per cent.

So, on 24 February 2003, the SEC filed criminal complaints against Mr Kittipat Yaoprukse and Roynet with the Economic Crime Investigation division of the Royal Thai Police (SEC, 24 February 2003). The police submitted the case to the Legal Proceeding Coordination Committee of the Ministry of Finance. Furthermore, the SET suspended the trading of Roynet's shares since January 2003 and blacklisted Mr Kittipat Yaoprukse, as a result of which he is barred for ten years from holding any director or senior management position of listed companies (Parnsoonthorn 2003).

On 28 February 2003, when Roynet held its annual general meeting, minority shareholders had gathered proxies to fire Mr Kittipat Yaoprukse as the managing director of Roynet. The board change required the approval of at least three-quarters of the people present at the meeting, which represented half of all shareholders' votes. Mr Kittipat Yaoprukse could not fight off the demands of the minority shareholders and resigned from his position as managing director (Parnsoonthorn 2003).

5.2 The Best Case: Electricity Generating Public Company Limited

Since the TRIS started rating companies on where they stand with regard to corporate governance, four companies have agreed to be rated. The results have been remarkable.

The Electricity Generating Public Company Limited (EGCO), the first independent power plant in Thailand, was established on 12 May 1992 through a partial shareholding of the Electricity Generating Authority of Thailand (EGAT). The EGCO was set up to help reduce the state enterprise's financial burden and encourage the private sector to invest in the energy industry, thereby increasing the efficiency of the electricity-generating business. EGCO produces electricity and supplies it to EGAT on a long-term purchase agreement along with helping EGAT search for good opportunities in the energy-related business.

EGCO scored 7.98 points on the full scale of 10 from TRIS, which is a "good-to-excellent" rating. The details of the four categories on which TRIS was rated are as follows:

- Shareholders' rights: 7.16 points. The shareholding structure of the company is clear and not complex and no cross-holding exists. The company allows shareholders to vote during the annual general meeting. The agenda of the meeting is clear and shareholders are given sufficient time to consider the agendas. The company allows the free expression of shareholders' opinions at the meeting.
- Composition and roles of board of directors and management: 7.6 points. The board of directors of the company consists of 13 members, four of whom are independent directors. The directors are well qualified, with different educational backgrounds and experience. The directors have an important role in defining the strategy of the company. The board has been placing emphasis on risk management since 2000 and has formed a work group for risk management. The board has also started a self-assessment programme.

- Information disclosure: 9.18 points. The company has an efficient disclosure system. Its financial statement passes the auditors without any problem. The company also releases the information regularly through various channels, for example, its website (www.egco.com), investors' relations unit, securities analysts' meeting. The company was one of the 40 best companies in non-financial disclosure, according to the rating of the SEC on 5 November 2002.
- Corporate governance culture: 8.16 points. The company has a policy of promoting good corporate governance at every level and it has formed work groups to disseminate information and arrange for training programmes to equip employees with a better understanding of corporate governance.

6. Future Challenges and Policy Recommendations

Since the financial crisis of 1997, Thailand has attempted to improve the corporate governance practice of listed firms through various voluntary and regulatory approaches. The Roynet case shows that greater efforts to improve corporate governance are required. The following are some recommendations for policy implementation:

- Strengthening legal enforcement: The Roynet case clearly shows that the current level of legal enforcement needs to be improved. Even though Thailand has sufficient laws to prosecute companies that do not adhere to the requirements of good corporate governance, any action that can possibly be taken has been slow in coming, leading the public to think that the authorities are not serious about its stand on good corporate governance. Recently, the SEC is considering changing the penalty from criminal code to civil code to accelerate the prosecution process.
- Legal enactment: Several significant laws concerning corporate governance are being revised, for example, the Securities and Exchange Commission Act and the Public Limited Company Act. The present version of these two laws, which are still in force, may not be adequate for enforcing corporate governance after the financial crisis. So, in fact, the government should appoint a committee to hasten the enactment of these corporate governance–related laws.

- Supporting research on corporate governance: Most of the research on corporate governance was done during 1996–98. As the Thai economy has undergone considerable restructuring since the crisis, much of the earlier research may no longer reflect the current situation. Future research in this area would be more useful if listed companies are subdivided into financial and non-financial ones. A comparison between the previous and future situations would serve as a guide to the directions that the government and supporting agencies should take to improve their policy on corporate governance. Other studies on corporate governance include studying the correlation, if any, between listed companies' stock prices and the initiatives they have undertaken to improve corporate governance, surveys on investor confidence in listed non-financial firms, content analyses of financial as well as non-financial disclosure in the annual report, and so forth.

- Continuity of corporate governance campaigns: After the financial crisis, several parties have attempted to increase public awareness and knowledge of corporate governance. Their efforts focus on the public at large to enable them to understand and take action when listed companies flout the rules. It would take a long time to achieve the desired behavioural outcome. Thus, it is important to continue the campaigns on good corporate governance.

- Integration on corporate governance efforts: Since there are several parties contributing to the good corporate governance campaigns, they should cooperate to ensure success. It has been noted that much has been done to improve corporate governance in Thailand, though most people are not aware of it. For the campaigns to be effective, co-ordination is necessary. The National Corporate Governance Committee is strategically placed to coordinate all these activities and publicize them on their website.

- Corporate responsibilities: In the long run, corporate governance is something that listed non-financial firms must be held accountable for to so as to be fair to its shareholders and stakeholders. Listed companies should act responsibly in this regard and not become a burden of the government or supporting agencies.

- Roles of minority shareholders: Ignorance of shareholders' rights has penalized minority shareholders severely during the financial crisis. In fact, when minority shareholders agree to join forces to take a certain position, they can be quite a force to reckon with, as witnessed in the Roynet case. Proper legal enforcement would gradually encourage minority shareholders to voice their opposition or take legal action against companies with poor corporate governance.

It is gratifying to know that there have been many success stories about companies striving to achieve good corporate governance in Thailand. Although legal enforcement can help ensure that companies abide by the rules, it is not always easy to punish the violaters. In this regard, the development of a self-monitoring system may be preferable to legal enforcement. But for this to be possible, there has to be public awareness and knowledge of what good corporate governance is.

Amidst the current economic improvement, Thailand is moving with caution for fear that the economic bubble will recur. An emphasis on good corporate governance practices would ensure that investors and the public are heading towards the right direction in its economic path.

REFERENCES

Alba, Pedro, Stijn Claessens, and Simeon Djankov. *Thailand's Corporate Financing and Governance Structures: Impact on Firms' Competitiveness*. Washington, DC: World Bank, May 1998.

Australian APEC Study Centre. *Corporate Governance in APEC: Rebuilding Asian Growth*. Symposium Report. December 1998. www.apec.org.au.

Organization for Economic Cooperation and Development. *OECD Principles of Corporate Governance*. Paris: OECD Publications, 1999.

Parnsoonthorn, Krissana. "Cornered Kittipat Quits". *Bangkok Post*, 1 March 2003, p. 1.

Price Waterhouse Management Consultants Ltd. *Corporate Governance in Thailand:. p- A Price Waterhouse Survey (Commissioned by the Stock Exchange of Thailand)*. Bangkok: Price Waterhouse, January 1997.

Stock Exchange of Thailand (SET). *The Roles, Duties and Responsibilities of the Directors of Listed Companies*. Bangkok: Boonsiri Printing, October 1998.

————. "Report on the Survey for Good Corporate Governance by the Committee of Good Corporate Governance Development". A report by the Working Committee in July 1999. In *Report on Corporate Governance*, pp. 34–43. Bangkok: Listing Department, Stock Exchange of Thailand, January 2000.

————. SET Vision 2003: International Standards of Enforcement and Corporate Governance. Bangkok: SET, June 2000.

————. *Code of Best Practice for Directors of Listed Companies*. Bangkok: Boonsiri Printing, October 1999a.

————. *Best Practice Guidelines for the Audit Committee*. Bangkok: Boonsiri Printing, October 1999b.

Thai Institute of Directors Association. Directors Certification Program. http://www.thai-iod.com. 2000.

————. *Strengthening Corporate Governance Practices in Thailand*. Bangkok, 2002.

World Bank, Thailand Office. *Thailand Economic Monitor*. http://www.worldbank.or.th/monitor. May 2003.

http://www.egco.co.th

http://www.roynet.co.th

http://www.sec.or.th/goodgov.index.shtml

http://www.sec.or.th/goodgov/progress.shtml

http://www.sec.or.th/goodgov/progres3.shtm

http://www.sec.or.th/secen1/legal/secact/newact.shtml

http://www.tris.co.th/products_services/governance_eng.html.

2

Good Governance in the Thai Banking System

Bhanupong Nidhiprabha

The Siam Commercial Bank Public Company Limited (SCB) and the Kasikornbank Public Company Limited (KBANK)[1] were the winners of the 2003 Board of the Year Awards. What had the two banks done (that other banks had not) to deserve the accolade? The KBANK was also one of the four winners of the corporate governance awards sponsored by the National Corporate Governance Committee (NCGC). In its assessment the Committee had assigned 20 per cent of the weightage to the companies' support of shareholders' rights. In addition, an independent audit committee of the bank was asked to submit its assessment directly to the board of directors.

According to the chairman of SCB, its practice of good governance has contributed to an improvement in the learning curve effect as well as a shortening of the response time to errors. In fact, it has been observed that good governance instils confidence in shareholders and builds stability as it can enhance investors' confidence. Some would even say that good governance can improve a firm's sustainability and help banks to survive in today's globalization. Such claims usually express some vague perceptions, or even wishful thinking, however, and are not backed up by facts. We need something more concrete to to establish the outcome from available evidence. To do so, we first have to quantify the degree of good governance put into practice. Second, we must be able to relate the indices of good governance to banks' performance indicators such as stock prices, non-performing loans, and profitability. Snapshots of these variables, before and after the shocks, can help us understand this complex relationship. Third, we must establish a channel through which good governance can transmit its impact on those performance indicators.

We must also not forget that banks' performance in terms of profitability and solvency can be affected by factors other than good governance. We must not naively echo the widely held view that good governance will result in better performance. This is because business cycle, appropriate management strategy and business policy, competitiveness, re-engineering, and many other factors also contribute to higher profits.

The key elements of good governance are transparency and accountability. After the currency crisis, Mr Rengchai Marakanond, the former Governor of the Bank of Thailand (BOT), was the only one who was taken to court. The BOT sued him for recklessness in using 185 billion baht to defend the Thai currency and to bail out financial institutions. But surely Mr Rengchai could not possibly be the only one responsible for the mismanagement of the financial policy? This is another example of lack of accountability.

However, all this is not surprising as Thailand's legal infrastructure is weak. The absence of accountability leads to moral hazard, which encourages further reckless behaviour. If bad bankers are not expected to pay for their white collar crimes, as is often the case, how could one expect any banker or his supervisors to be held responsible for their oversight and reckless behaviour? Whatever their intentions, they do not have to pay for the damage that results from their reckless behaviour.

The rest of this chapter is organized as follows. Section 1 examines the level of corporate governance in three Thai banks belonging to the group of the top 25 banks in terms of good governance in Asia. The international ranking in 2002 was conducted by Credit Lyonnais Securities Asia Limited (CLSA). Section 2 analyses the relationship between good governance and banks' stock performance. Section 3 reviews market regulations on banking governance. Section 4 concludes the chapter.

1. An International Comparison among Asian Banks

In the CLSA annual ranking of emerging markets for corporate governance in 2002 (Figure 2.1), only three Thai banks are included among the top 25 in the Asian banking sector: SCB, TFB (now KBANK), and Bangkok Bank Public Company Limited (BBL). The three banks are among the big four Thai banks; the fourth bank not included in the CLSA list is the Krung Thai Bank Public Company Limited (KTB), which is a state-owned enterprise. The fact that KTB is not included is not surprising as the public bank has been employed by the Thai government to pursue specific public policies such as the taking over of other ailing banks. Questions also arise as to the relationship between a bank's size and its conduct of good banking practice. Does size matter? Is it true that small banks cannot afford to do the right thing?

SCB, the bank that scores highest in corporate governance in Thailand, ranks seventeenth among the top 25 banks in Asia — far behind five Hong Kong banks, four Malaysian banks, four Korean banks, and three Singaporean banks. So, there is a lot yet to be done — not to mention other laggards in the Thai banking sector, some of which are still struggling with non-performing loans. Table 2.1 presents a breakdown of the score details of the three Thai banks compared with other Asian banks included in the top 25. It is noted that the CLSA ranking is carried out for corporations in general and not confined to commercial banks. One conclusion to be drawn from the CLSA ranking is that countries with better corporate governance outperform in their stock markets, while countries with worse corporate governance have dreadful market performance in terms of the dollar rate of return.

SCB came out top among Thai banks with a 63.4 per cent score, followed by TFB and BBL at 58.2 per cent and 54.7 per cent, respectively.

Figure 2.1
Good Banking Governance Scores in Asia, 2002

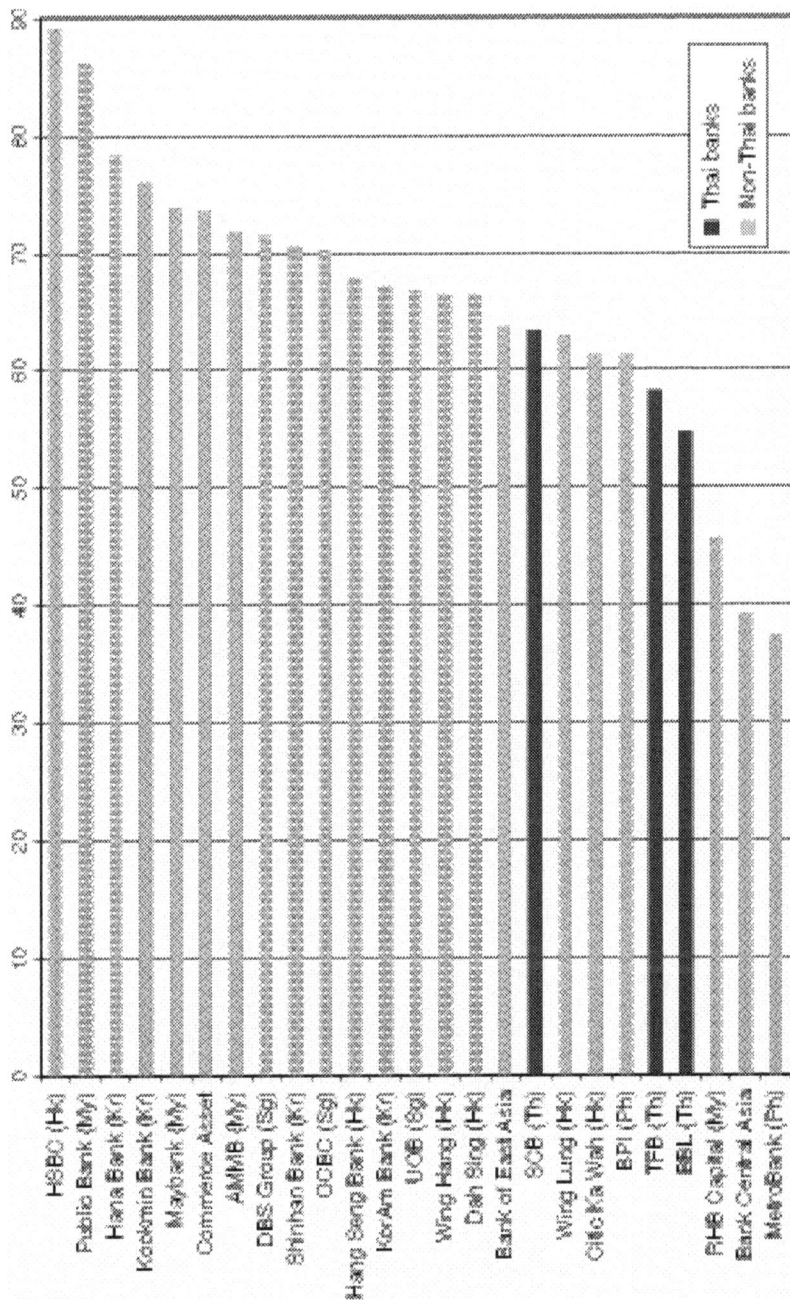

Legend: ■ Thai banks ▨ Non-Thai banks

Banks (top to bottom): HSBC (HK), Public Bank (M), Hana Bank (Kr), Kookmin Bank (Kr), Maybank (M), Commerce Asset, AMMB (M), DBS Group (Sg), Shinhan Bank (Kr), OCBC (Sg), Hang Seng Bank (HK), Kor Am Bank (Kr), UOB (Sg), Wing Hang (HK), Dah Sing (HK), Bank of East Asia, SCB (Th), Wing Lung (HK), Citic Ka Wah (HK), BPI (Ph), TFB (Th), BBL (Th), RHB Capital (M), Bank Central Asia, MetroBank (Ph)

Source: Compiled from CLSA Ranking of Emerging Markets for Corporate Governance (2002).

Table 2.1

Breakdown of Scores Attained in Various Aspects of Corporate Governance: Thai Banks Compared with Other Asian Banks, 2002

Bank	Total (100%)	Discipline (15%)	Transparency (15%)	Independence (15%)	Accountability (15%)	Responsibility (15%)	Fairness (15%)	Social Awareness (10%)
BBL (Th)	54.7	44.4	80.0	50.0	62.5	33.3	50.0	66.6
SCB (Th)	63.4	55.5	90.0	75.0	75.0	33.3	50.0	66.6
TFB (Th)	58.2	55.5	80.0	50.0	75.0	33.3	50.0	66.6
HSBC (Hk)	89.1	100.0	80.0	92.9	87.5	66.7	100.0	100.0
Hang Seng Bank (Hk)	67.9	55.6	80.0	64.3	75.0	50.0	83.3	66.7
Dah Sing (Hk)	66.4	33.3	70.0	64.3	75.0	66.7	88.9	66.7
Bank of East Asia (Hk)	63.7	33.3	70.0	64.3	62.5	66.7	83.3	66.7
Wing Hang (Hk)	66.4	33.3	70.0	64.3	75.0	66.7	88.9	66.7
Citic Ka Wah (Hk)	61.2	33.3	70.0	64.3	62.5	50.0	83.3	66.7
Wing Lung (Hk)	62.9	33.3	70.0	64.3	62.5	66.7	77.8	66.7
Bank Central Asia (Id)	39.2	33.3	80.0	37.5	12.5	16.7	70.0	16.7
Public Bank (My)	86.1	77.8	70.0	100.0	87.5	83.3	100.0	83.3
Maybank (My)	73.8	77.8	70.0	100.0	50.0	66.7	83.3	66.7
Commerce Asset (My)	73.6	100.0	70.0	100.0	87.5	50.0	38.9	66.7
AMMB (My)	71.7	77.8	70.0	92.9	37.5	66.7	88.9	66.7
RHB Capital (My)	45.7	77.8	70.0	42.9	25.0	50.0	44.4	66.7
BPI (Ph)	61.2	55.6	62.5	78.6	80.0	20.0	66.7	66.7
Metrobank (Ph)	37.4	33.3	50.0	21.4	60.0	40.0	11.1	50.0
DBS Group (Sg)	71.4	66.7	90.0	92.9	37.5	50.0	83.3	83.3
UOB (Sg)	66.7	66.7	90.0	78.6	37.5	33.3	83.3	83.3
OCBC (Sg)	70.1	77.8	90.0	85.7	25.0	50.0	83.3	83.3
KorAm Bank (Kr)	67.1	55.6	80.0	64.3	75.0	33.3	94.4	66.7
Hana Bank (Kr)	78.2	66.7	80.0	92.9	87.5	50.0	100.0	66.7
Kookmin Bank (Kr)	76.0	44.4	100.0	85.7	87.5	50.0	94.4	66.7
Shinhan bank (Kr)	70.7	44.4	80.0	78.5	62.5	50.0	100.0	83.3

Note: Hk = Hong Kong; Id = Indonesia; Kr = Korea; My = Malaysia; Ph = Philippines; Th = Thailand; Sg = Singapore.
Source: Compiled from *CLSA Ranking of Emerging Markets for Corporate Governance* (2002).

The three Thai banks are weakest in the category of "responsibility", outperforming one bank only — Bank of the Philippines Islands (BPI) — in this area (Table 2.1). The three banks obtain the same 33.3 per cent on the responsibility index, which indicates that their boards and senior management share the same low level of responsibility for their shareholders. An agency problem exists when management and shareholders have a conflict of interests because of different goals and ideas on how the bank should be run. Thus the agency problem still remains substantial. Some of the issues that Thai banks may have scored poorly in are: whether the persons responsible for flagrant business failures or misdemeanours are appropriately punished; whether the board has taken measures to safeguard the interests of all and not just of the dominant shareholders; whether any action can be taken against the management committee in the event of mismanagement; whether the board is small enough (not more than 12) to be effective and efficient. It is noted that the score of each of the three Thai banks under the category of responsibility to shareholders is only half that of the Hong Kong and Shanghai Banking Corporation Limited (HSBC). The top governance bank in Asia, with the highest score of 83.3 per cent in this category goes to Public Bank Berhad (Public Bank) of Malaysia. Sad to say, it may be difficult for Thai banks to improve in this area because of the existing corporate culture and the social code of conduct.

Another area Thai commercial banks are weak in is the independence of the board. It is difficult for family-owned banks to have a chairman who is an independent, non-executive director. Thai banks fail in the independence category partly because their management committee is not substantially different from members of the board and major shareholders dominate the management committee. Many Thai banks also lag behind their Asian counterparts in that they do not have an independent audit committee, a remuneration committee, and a nominating committee. Nevertheless, in December 2002, the Bank of Thailand (BOT) had laid down guidelines for setting up these three independent committees. Moreover, the number of the board members must be at least nine, with a minimum of three independent members, and at most one-third of the seats can be filled by bank executives. One cannot pretend that the senior management have not in the recent five years made decisions that are favourable to themselves at the expense of shareholders. As shown in Table 2.1, the BBL and TFB have achieved only 50 per cent of the level of good governance attained by the Public Bank, the Malayan Banking Berhad (Maybank), and the Commerce Asset-Holding Berhad (CAHB) of Malaysia. Any improvement in their corporate governance will only be visible in 2003 after the new guidelines of the BOT are voluntarily adopted by all commercial banks in Thailand.[2]

On the issue of transparency, Asian banks generally score very high, thanks to the Asian financial crisis, which continues to remind them of the importance of full disclosure. The SCB has even outperformed HSBC in terms of transparency, achieving 90 per cent of the total score. The three Thai banks regularly publish clear and informative annual reports; they provide timely market-sensitive information with up-to-date data; their accounts are presented according to the International Generally Accepted Accounting Principles (IGAAP); analysts have good access to the senior management. Viewed in this light, banks are willing to disclose their sensitive information as the benefit of being transparent far outweighs the cost. Asymmetric information is not a major issue here.

If the banks truly realize the importance of good governance, they must issue a mission statement indicating clearly the priority they place on good governance, and their annual report must include a section on how their principle is implemented. In order to solve the problem of moral hazard, the senior management must be given incentive to work towards a higher share price of the bank. When there is no incompatibility of incentives between the principal and their agents, bank executives will not misbehave. This is how the CLSA based its evaluation of the banks. In addition, banks that exercise good behaviour should not engage in non-core business or mobilize funds at the cost of equity that is excessively higher than the required rate of return for them to remain viable. Banks that observe strict financial discipline will not engage in reckless lending that could jeopardize the returns to their shareholders. Discipline is meant to curb any possible excessive risk-taking by the management. The top three Thai banks still lag behind HSBC and all five Malaysian banks in the list of top corporate governance banks shown in Table 2.1.

The top three governance Thai banks performed relatively well in the area of accountability, where an audit committee nominate and review the work of external auditors, supervising both internal auditors and accounting procedures. In the near future when the number of independent, non-executive directors accounts for more than 66 per cent of the board — according to new guidelines of the BOT — the accountability of the board will be greatly enhanced. Note that the sheer number of the independent board members is not as important as the functions they undertake. Apart from being appointed by the nomination of non-major shareholders, they must have a record of voting on certain issues against the rest of the board in order to be considered as non-executive directors who are demonstrably and unquestionably independent.

Thai banks perform poorly on the category of fairness, scoring only half of what HSBC has attained and outperforming only the CAHB of Malaysia and the Metropolitan Bank and Trust Company (Metrobank) of the Philippines. What has gone wrong? The fact that the best governance banks in Thailand can achieve only 50 per cent of the total score indicates that there is plenty of room for improvement in the area of fairness. The majority shareholders are believed to have gained at the expense of minority shareholders. Furthermore, not all equity shareholders have the right to call general meetings. Although all the relevant information is made available prior to the general meeting, the majority shareholders as a group own more than 40 per cent of the banks, in particular the hybrid banks originating from the foreign takeover of troubled domestic banks. Furthermore, the total remuneration to directors seems to have increased faster than the net profit over the recent five years.

Some of the criteria of social awareness adopted by CLSA seem to be more related to other business undertakings than banking operations, except for the explicit public policy statements emphasizing strict ethical codes of conduct rather than observance according to the letter of the law. Other aspects of social awareness such as environmental consciousness or operation in Myanmar are totally irrelevant, while that on equal employment opportunities and promotion is valid.

Table 2.2 summarizes the data in Table 2.1, focusing on the performance of Thai banks relative to the performance of the benchmark bank — the United Overseas Bank Limited (UOB) of Singapore, which obtained the median score of 66.7 per cent. The maximum total score

Table 2.2
Corporate Governance of Thai Banks in 2002: Strengths and Weaknesses

	Total	Discipline	Transparency	Independence	Accountability	Responsibility	Fairness	Social Awareness
			Relative Scores Compared with the Median (UOB)					
BBL (Th)	0.67	0.89	0.64	1.67	1.00	0.60	0.79	0.82
SCB (Th)	0.83	1.00	0.95	2.00	1.00	0.60	0.79	0.95
TFB (Th)	0.83	0.89	0.64	2.00	1.00	0.60	0.79	0.87

Source: Compiled from CLSA *Ranking of Emerging Markets for Corporate Governance* (2002).

of 89.1 per cent went to HSBC, while Metrobank of the Philippines received the lowest score — 37.4 per cent. If the number in any cell in Table 2.2 exceeds unity, it implies that the particular Thai bank had outperformed the UOB. If the number is less than one, however, it implies that the relevant bank had underperformed in that category. As indicated in the table, SCB, BBL, and TFB outperformed UOB on "accountability" and were on par with UOB in terms of responsibility to shareholders. But the three Thai banks tailed behind other banks in the category of good governance. All three banks achieved only 60 per cent of what UOB attained in terms of responsibility of the management to shareholders. As such, the agency problem remains blatantly unresolved. Nevertheless, the agency cost might have been exaggerated when there was a large concentration of ownership. Thus any effort to raise the score on responsibility governance will not help in the short run as long as income and wealth distribution remains largely unaffected by economic development.

Although the ranking of CLSA provides vital information on corporate governance of only the top three Thai banks, it serves as an upper bound or the maximum achievable level of the Thai banking sector. Other Thai banks, including some hybrid banks, must have performed very poorly, well below the standard set by these three banks at all levels of governance. Thus we may conclude that although the BOT has attempted to issue guidelines for good governance in the banking industry in line with international standards, a lot of work is still required to ensure that the guidelines are implemented according to international best practices.

2. Good Governance and Bank Stock Prices

There has been a growing body of literature on the impact of top management changes on stock prices. Fama and Jensen (1983) hypothesize that there would be a positive effect on stock prices when it is announced that internal directors are appointed as board members. The underlying assumption is that the internal directors of a firm are more familiar with its operation than external board members. Brickly et al. (1994), however, argue that the appointment of external directors would contribute to incentive-alignment between management and shareholders. As such, with regard to good governance in the banking industry, firms that have a policy of appointing more independent outside directors would be favoured by investors.

For institutional investors, banks with good governance are often preferred, other things being equal, to banks that have no genuine commitment to good governance principles. Institutional investors' preferences are different from those of retail domestic investors, who tend to have a shorter time horizon. The fact is that doing the right thing would only pay off in the long run. As retail investors are generally attracted by short-term gains, they are more likely to respond to rumours and hearsay and join the herd. Whether the practice of good governance will enhance a bank's stock price also depends on the proportion of market players who disregard the importance of corporate governance.

The year 2000 was the year that the Thai stock market went through its trough, experiencing a reduction of more than 40 per cent. See Figures 2.2a and 2.2b. Badly shaken by the financial crisis in 1997, bank shares fell miserably, plunging greater depths than the SET index. However, during the rebound, BBL, TFB, and SCB outperformed the SET (Figure 2.2a), while the shares of other Thai banks — which were not considered "good governance" banks — did not recover as much as the percentage gained by the SET. The only exception was the share of the Bank of Ayudhya Public Company Limited (BAY), which has continued to outperform the market since 2002.

In another survey conducted by the Thai Institute of Directors Association (IOD) and the McKinsey & Company in 2000, BAY was among the six banks listed as the top 50 companies that upgraded their practice of corporate governance. Other banks included in the list were the DBS Thai Danu Bank Public Company Limited (DTDB), the Krung Thai Bank Public Company Limited (KTB), the Thanachart Bank Public Company Limited, the Thai Farmers Bank Public Company Limited (TFB), and the Siam Commercial Bank Public Company Limited (SCB). The criteria utilized by the CLSA were different from the ones employed by the IOD, which were based on the rights of shareholders, the role of stakeholders in corporate governance, disclosure and transparency, and board responsibilities. Not all of these six banks managed to raise their

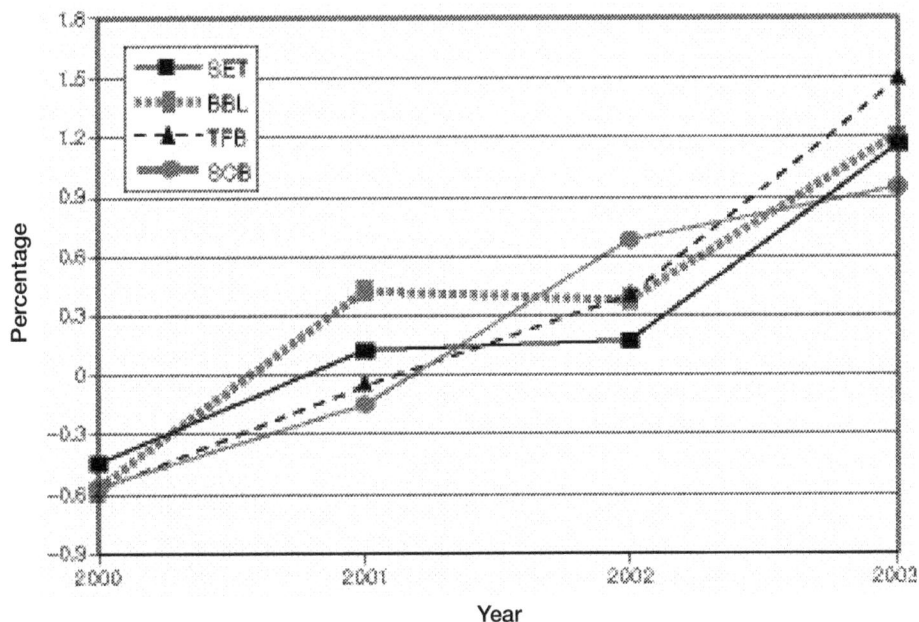

Figure 2.2a
Share Prices of Good Governance Thai Banks
(Percentage Change)

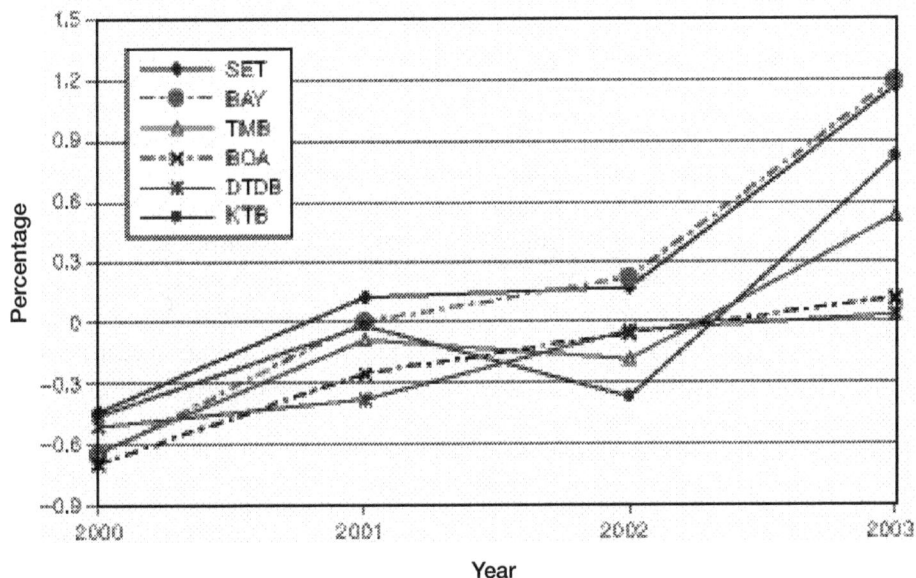

Figure 2.2b
Share Prices of Other Thai Banks
(Percentage Change)

share prices above the market trend. KTB and DTDB performed poorly relative to the SET index (Figure 2.2b).

During the market slump in 2000, bank shares suffered a sharper drop in values than other sectors did. Nevertheless, as indicated by Table 2.3, the share prices of the top three "good governance" banks suffered less than those of other banks during the downturn from 1995 to 2000. And on the upturn, the share prices of the three banks rebounded more quickly than other banks. Because of the takeover by foreign banks, BOA and DTDB did not suffer as sharp a decline in their share prices as other banks did. The figures shown in Table 2.3 employed the share values in 2000 as a benchmark. The data for 2003 are based on stock prices at the end of June 2003. Whether share prices can exhibit a remarkable rebound during the recovery or whether they have some ability to resist the impact of the bear market also depends on the intrinsic value of the individual bank, which in turn depends on its reputation and franchise value, as well as its size and market capitalization. Big banks with large market capitalization are generally less easily influenced by share manipulation.

Figures 2.3a and 2.3b provide information on the asset quality of Thai commercial banks between 1995 and 2003. Figure 2.3a indicates that the accrued interest receivables of "good governance" banks were well below 1 per cent, whereas those of banks not included in the good governance club had a higher percentage of lower-quality loans. The sharp declines in the accrued interest receivables, as observed in Figure 2.3b, were the result of bad debt write-offs and capital injection by foreign banks, that is, DBS, Standard Chartered,[3] OUB, and ABN Amro. When information on quality of assets becomes transparent, as required for good governance compliance, the share prices would reflect the true values of the banks. Thus, transparency allows investors to distinguish between good and bad banks. When "bad" banks adopt the policy of transparency, they are more likely to see their share prices decline than previously when they were able to conceal their problems by cosmetic management. Transparency and upgrading of accounting standards to full disclosure therefore can have both positive and negative impacts on share prices.

Table 2.3
Performance of Thai Banks' Stock Prices Relative to Their Values, 2000

	1995	1996	1997	1998	1999	2000	2001	2002	2003
SET	4.75801	3.08915	1.38448	1.32178	1.79026	1	1.12875	1.32426	2.86842
BBL	8.47058	7.49019	3.37254	2.03921	2.39215	1	1.43137	1.94117	4.27451
TFB	5.83282	4.23897	2.03487	1.81435	2.20512	1	0.95384	1.33333	3.33333
SCB	11.83646	8.01822	2.43038	0.88607	2.25316	1	0.85063	1.43038	2.78481
BAY	21.17358	11.32075	3.77358	2.12264	2.87735	1	1.00000	1.21698	2.66037
TMB	15.03653	8.72809	1.72833	1.67647	2.72213	1	0.91818	0.74909	1.14531
BOA	6.67868	4.37509	1.38245	3.22475	3.24810	1	0.74329	0.69736	0.77817
DTDB	4.30373	5.00204	1.47361	1.64819	2.03313	1	0.62650	0.60241	0.62650
KTB	9.67441	4.65116	0.91162	1.83720	1.83720	1	0.98604	0.62325	1.13488

Source: Stock Exchange of Thailand.

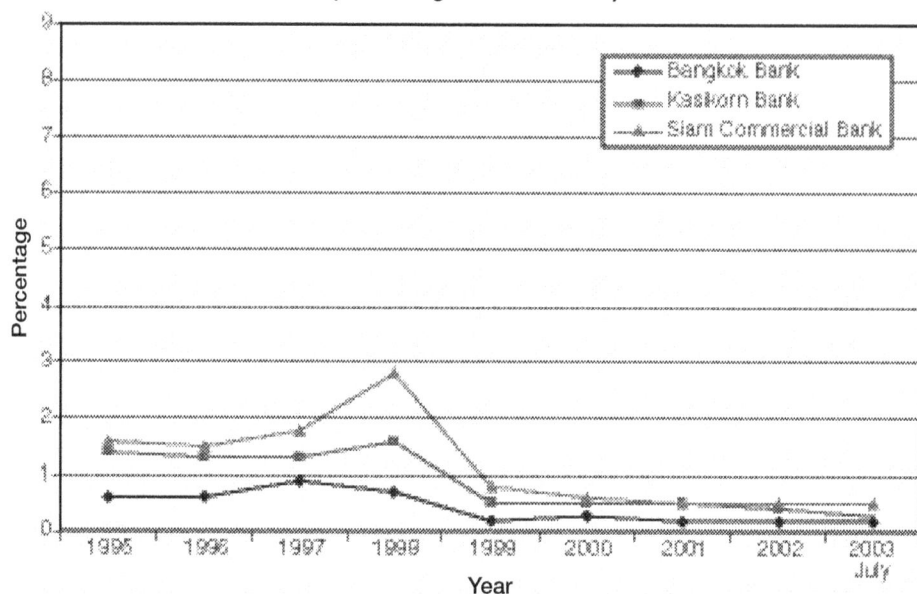

Figure 2.3a
Accrued Interest Receivables of Good Governance Banks
(Percentage of Total Loans)

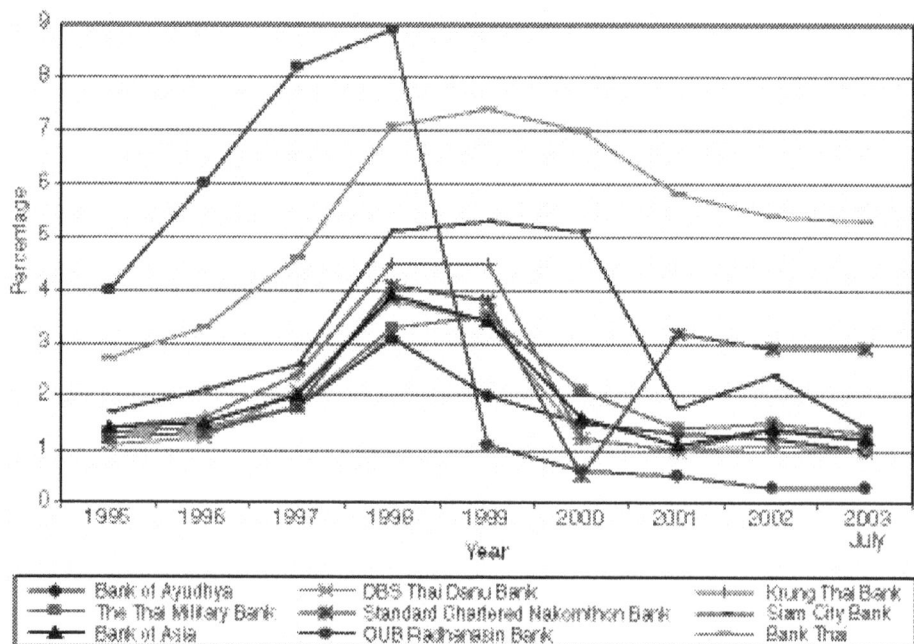

Figure 2.3b
Accrued Interest Receivables of Other Thai Banks
(Percentage of Total Loans)

We might conclude that unless good governance is directly related to banks' performance in the short run, there is no concrete evidence supporting the view that the share prices of good governance banks outperform the share prices of banks that score lower on good governance. Successful banks can afford the luxury of good governance compliance. But compliance itself may have been a result of rules imposed by market regulators rather than something arising out of a genuine desire to do the right thing as well as to be credible.

So we should not be hasty and jump into the conclusion that the share price of good governance banks will always outperform those of "not-so-good-governance" banks. The correlation does not necessarily imply causality as there could be a third factor linking share prices and the practice of good governance, with share prices and good governance themselves being only remotely related. Even if they are causally related, the causation could run both ways. Share prices can be seen as the present values of expected capital gains and dividend pay-offs. Any above-average capital gain earned by the shares of good governance banks could reflect the expected profitability of banks, whose operations are driven by efficient management. In other words, good governance is just one factor among many that can influence stock prices.

3. Market Regulations and Good Governance

Insider lending leads to poor loan quality. For foreign-controlled banks, the loans made to related political parties as a percentage of their total loans are relatively low and the percentage seems to be declining (Figure 2.4a). The four hybrid banks, whose majority shareholders are foreign banks, do not engage much in lending to their related parties (insider lending). The proportion of such loans extended by the four hybrid banks was extremely low compared with that extended by the Thai banks (Figure 2.4b). The Thai Military Bank Public Company Limited, which has difficulty selling its shares to foreign buyers, is among the large banks associated with insider lending. Both TFB and BAY are the best performers in this category. Although it is very difficult for BBL and SCB not to lend to their related parties, the situation has improved and the trend has been encouraging.

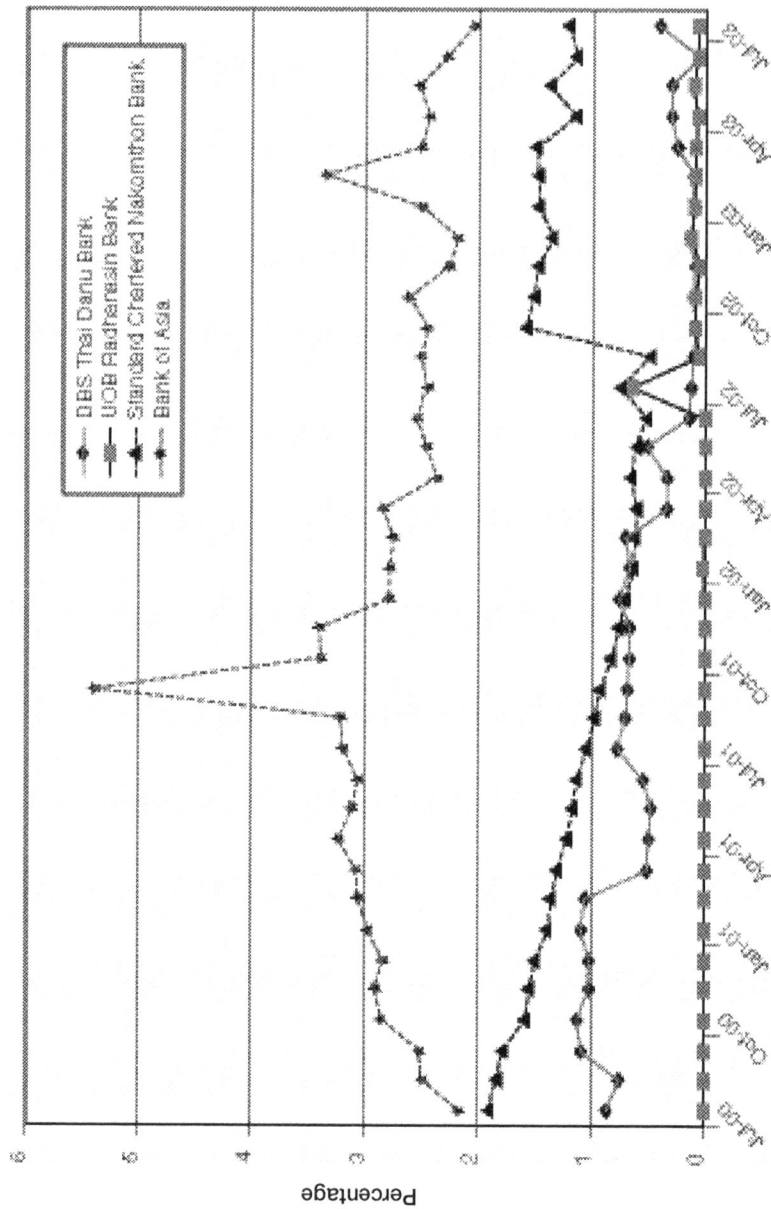

Figure 2.4a
Loan to Related Parties of Foreign-Controlled Banks

Figure 2.4b

Loan to Related Parties of Good Governance Banks and Other Private Banks

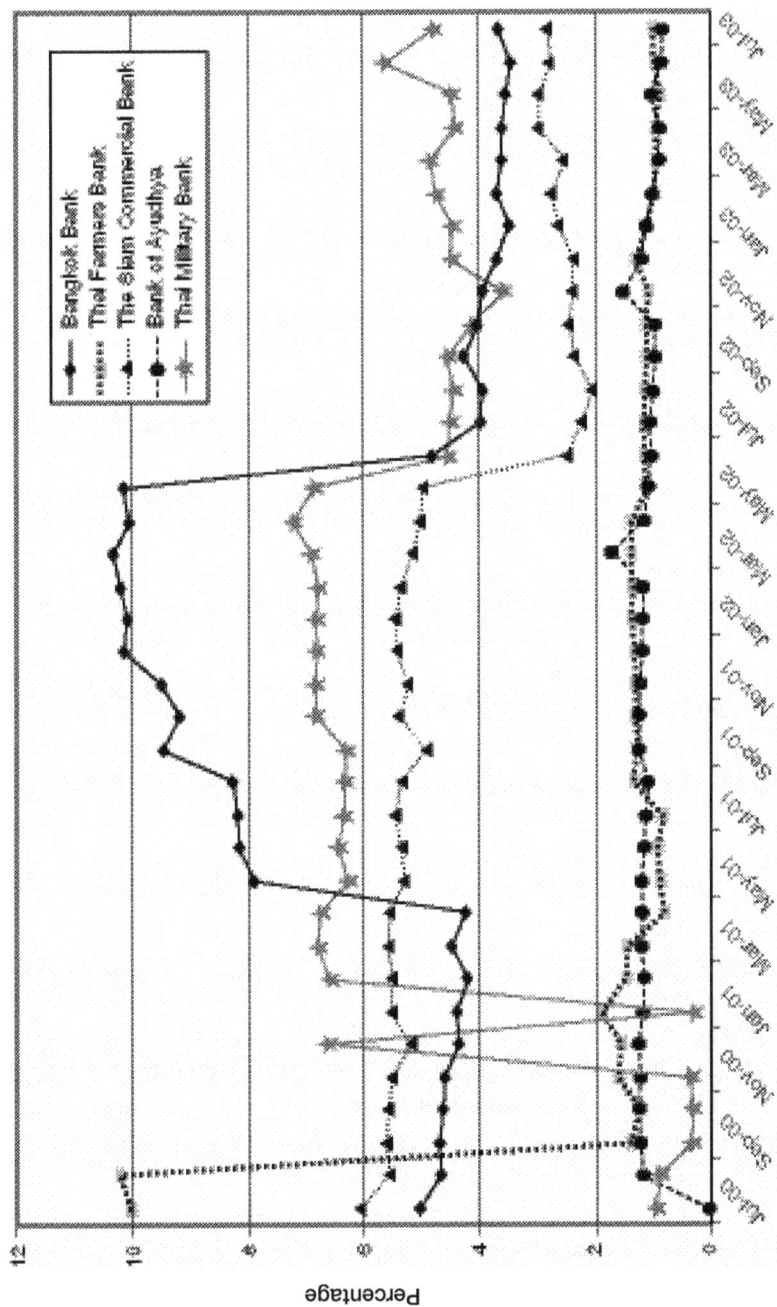

With the strong economic growth in 2003, SCB is the first private bank that has paid dividends since the financial crisis, while its first-tier capital has reached 9.5 per cent of its risk-weighted assets, exceeding the Basle Accord requirement of 8 per cent. The attempt to push forward the adoption of the Basle Accord II, which goes beyond capital adequacy ratio into market risks standard, might be thwarted as long as the remaining weak banks are still struggling with their non-performing loans. Even the largest bank — BBL — was stuck with non-performing loans of 25 per cent of its total loans at the end of 2003. Thai banks need time to unload their non-performing assets. Any attempt to speed up the rules and regulations might be counter-productive in terms of macroeconomic impact as long as the real sector requires credit from commercial banks.

The literature on good governance stresses the importance of reducing agency conflicts. According to Flannery (1994), the higher leverage in the banking industry has magnified the impact of managerial actions on shareholder wealth. Hence, the main purpose of corporate governance is to protect the interest of shareholders. Having an independent board to monitor management can reduce the divergence of incentives between management and shareholders. As the evidence provided by Saunders et al. (1990) indicates, ownership structure affects the amount of risk-taking activities of commercial banks. The implication of the finding is that banks will be less adventurous when the management has a lot to lose from undertaking risky lending.

In developing countries where many banks are family-owned and the banks are run by family members who are also large shareholders, the problem of agency conflict will not be as severe as in the case of banks with a less concentrated ownership. Booth et al. (2002) provides convincing evidence from the United States that as long as bank regulations can reduce the impact of managerial decisions on shareholder wealth, internal monitoring mechanisms such as increasing the percentage of external directors and providing directors with stock ownership become less important in controlling agency conflicts.

Although shareholder wealth can be enhanced after successfully seducing cross-border investors into town by waving the good governance banner, there are much more important benefits from wholeheartedly embracing good governance practices.

The cause of the financial crisis of 1997 has often been attributed to the lack of good governance. This may seem like overstating the importance of good governance and underestimating the role of other possible contributing factors. For instance, one should not rule out the fact that the main culprit could well be the unsustainable exchange rate policy in the 1990s.

But if good governance is doing the right thing and being credible, there might be some grain of truth in the statement. An important positive outcome of good governance in the banking system is that it reduces vulnerabilities to shocks in the banking sector. As argued by Litan et al. (2002), the area that has received too little attention is the extent to which financial crises have resulted from a failure in "governance" broadly defined to include effective management of public institutions and private firms. In the case of Thailand, monitoring agencies, accounting firms, and auditors are not subject to as severe punishments as they should be when they make errors, whether intentionally or unintentionally.

Thailand is still a predominantly bank-based economy, although equity and bond markets have become increasingly important as sources of funds. There will always be asymmetry in information for bankers and their clients. And if the stock market is not efficient, it will not be able to solve the problem of asymmetric information and moral hazard. If this is the case, then it cannot be said that a bank-based economy necessarily has a less efficient allocation of resources than the capital market. Good governance through transparency and accountability in both lenders and borrowers can improve efficiency in the allocation of financial resources. Thus regulations are needed to ensure transparency, accountability, and predictability.

According to Borio (2003), bank regulations can be sub-divided into two components. The micro-prudential element is to avoid problems that can be encountered by individual banks by limiting risk exposure through the capital adequacy requirement. When a problem occurs with an individual bank that might spread to other banks, the micro-prudential approach can nip the problem in the bud and stop it from affecting the whole system. The second component of regulations is the macro-prudential element, which has often not been given due emphasis. When all the banks in a country are exposed to the same risks, systemic crises can be triggered by the outbreak of a common shock such as a devaluation. The financial system can be more stable if regulations can be put in place to patch up vulnerabilities in the banking system and thus limit the damage to the economy. Prompt corrective actions using the macro-prudential approach are needed to tighten capital requirements in economic booms and to ease them in the slumps.

Good governance does not only apply to commercial banks and other financial firms; it must also be applied to the regulatory bodies, which form an integral part of the banking system. Regulators must establish prompt corrective actions and adhere to a proper code of conduct. Just as commercial banks are required to be transparent and accountable, the central banks must also show transparency and accountability. That is, they must practise what they preach.

The BOT in 2000 followed the global trend of good corporate governance by imposing regulations on commercial banks. Transparency is one of the requirements, and commercial banks are required to disclose information in the following areas: non-performing loans, loans to related parties, and any violation against the BOT's regulations. The amount of a bank's lending to related companies is limited to less than 50 per cent of shareholder equity, or 25 per cent of the total liabilities of the companies, or 5 per cent of tier-one capital of the bank, whichever is lower. In addition, to minimize conflict of interests, bank directors and senior executives are not permitted to sit on the board of more than three other companies (Bank of Thailand 2000).

In December 2002, the BOT issued new guidelines for the board of directors of commercial banks: the number of executive directors must not exceed one-third of the members on the board. The board must have at least three independent directors or at least 25 per cent of the total number of members on the board. In addition, commercial banks must establish the following: (a) an audit committee with at least three directors, two of whom must be independent; (b) a risk-management committee with at least five members from the board of directors; and

(c) a nominating committee to select directors and a remuneration committee to review compensation of bank executives and directors. By July 2002 the BOT had tightened the rules further by prohibiting banks from lending to directors, their families, and their companies if they hold a stake of more than 30 per cent in the bank (Bank of Thailand 2002).

Good governance requires both the legal infrastructure as well as the realization that it is beneficial in the long run: the practice of good governance is vital to the sustainability of the organization. The insolvency and foreclosure laws are ineffective and do not help strengthen the market infrastructure. In the United States the insolvency law is favourable to debtors, while in the United Kingdom and Japan, it offers protection to creditors. As long as Thailand has a significant number of strategic borrowers who refuse to pay up their debts even though they are able to, any improvement in law enforcement, including the strengthening of the foreclosure law, can greatly enhance the practice of good governance.

4. Concluding Remarks

As long as the management in the banking industry and shareholders do not believe in the importance of good governance, the Thai banking industry will not be able to reach international standards of best practices. Trillions of dollars of investment funds from multinational institutional investors may be attractive enough for local banks to unwillingly adopt some of the measures of good governance. Rules and regulations may be further imposed to ensure transparency, accountability, and fairness. Good banking governance, similar to any ethical code, is useful if it is widely accepted by the banking community. In fact, adherence to the principles of good governance is good for everybody. Because of asymmetric information arising from the lack of transparency, good banks and their shareholders suffer from undervalued shares, while bad banks and their owners profit from the unfair advantage. As Arrow (1973) warned us 30 years ago, firms ought not solely pursue profit maximization; social responsibility should also be taken into account. In the banking industry, asymmetric information is a major problem, and public confidence is the most important intangible asset of commercial banks. When the impact of negative externality can be so severe that a run on a single bank may lead to a systemic banking failure, it is of utmost importance to institutionalize social responsibility. Regulations could be imposed with a credible threat of legal liability. Again, the punishment for violation of ethical rules must be severe enough to deter moral hazard. In addition, the banking community itself must establish internal pressures for accepting and upholding the esteem of good banking governance.

The Thai economy is expected to experience sustained economic growth over the next three years. What can be a better time than now to strengthen the rules of good governance in the banking sector? According to a new state initiative to buy non-performing assets from local financial institutions, Thai bankers will no longer be saddled with large amounts of non-performing assets. Local banks can unload their 700 billion baht foreclosed non-performing loans to state-owned asset management companies and resume their normal lending activities. The strong economic recovery is a crucial transition period since bankers may suffer from disaster myopia and a short memory. Rules of good banking governance should be strengthened to guard against the bad behaviour rampant during the last boom. Bankers have to change their mindset before they can change their behaviour to voluntarily comply with regulations.

As far as fairness is concerned, the majority shareholders should not gain at the expense of the minority shareholders. The same rule of fairness should be applied to both commercial banks and their regulators. The BOT has done a great deal in promoting transparency of its activities through its website. International investors have regained confidence in the effectiveness of Thailand's monetary policy, which has been enhanced by the independence of the central bank after the financial crisis. What is still needed is accountability. In future, when commercial banks fail or when the inflation target is missed, the rule of accountability and responsibility that regulators require of commercial banks must apply equally to the central bank. Is there any mechanism to allow for the punishment of the management in the event of a mismanagement of the country's monetary and financial policies?

The lack of an effective legal infrastructure hinders the practice of good corporate governance. As long as the wrongdoing of players in the banking industry, including strategic borrowers, go unpunished the observance of good governance in the banking system may just be a fashionable thing to do to appease investors — something similar to the ISO 9000 and the like. As the research works of Claessens et al. (1999) and La Porta et al. (1998) show, the degree of enforcement of the judicial system in terms of rule of law, corruption, risk of expropriation, and risk of contract repudiation remains relatively low in Thailand. The level of enforcement in the Thai judicial system was 62.7 per cent that of Japan, 76 per cent that of Malaysia, and 88 per cent that of the Republic of Korea. At the same time, the top 15 families in Thailand owned 53 per cent of market capitalization, compared with corresponding figures of 38 per cent in Korea, 28 per cent in Malaysia, and 2.8 per cent in Japan. Because of the negative relationship between wealth concentration and the level of judicial enforcement, it is a very difficult task for market regulators to instil and inspire the concept of good governance without first dismantling the monopolistic structure of corporations and their close relationships with commercial banks. The rule of law may be easily broken. Laws that encourage market competition and market discipline are not likely to be passed.

The importance of providing a market-friendly environment and competition cannot be understated. With the intense pressure to open up the banking sector to foreign competition, the Thai banking sector will become more consolidated in the future. This will enable Thailand to exploit economies of scale so that it can compete effectively with foreign banks. It means that Thailand should create a good banking culture to survive in the new competitive environment. No longer should the government intervene to shore up ailing banks.[4] Intervention in the banking sector should be reduced. As long as there are state-owned banks, it is unlikely that Thai banks would pursue their own goals of maximizing profits for their shareholders. The government-owned banks are used as a channel for the government to conduct its policy. The Government Savings Bank, KTB, and the Siam City Bank Public Company Limited are required to lend to the Oil Fund at the prescribed rates of interest to finance the government's policy of maintaining unrealistically low prices of oil to suppress expectations of inflation in the face of rising prices of crude oil. So it looks like good governance in the Thai banking sector will have to await the complete privatization of state-owned banks.

In a survey on corporate governance, Shleifer and Vishny (1997) reckons that corporate governance deals with the ways in which suppliers of finance to corporations assure themselves of a return on their investment. That view can be regarded as a narrow view of corporate governance. When dealing with the banking industry, where the adverse impacts of the players in the markets are large and detrimental to the health of the whole economy, a broader view of corporate governance that includes social responsibility is called for. Responsibility at the macro level is required from all players in the industry — the regulators, bankers, auditors, monitoring agencies, depositors — to recognize moral hazard and be ready to blow the whistle when necessary.

NOTES

1. Formerly known as Thai Farmers Bank Public Co. Ltd. (TFB). The change involved the English version of the name only, which now uses only one word "Kasikornbank" in English. This is not only concise but is also compatible with the pronunciation of the bank's name in Thai. The bank registered its new English name with the Ministry of Commerce, Thailand, on 4 April 2003. The bank also asked for its stock code on the Stock Exchange of Thailand to be changed from "TFB" to "KBANK".

2. In a survey published by the World Bank in 2005, more than two-thirds of Thai listed companies can meet international corporate governance standards. Thailand adopted Corporate Governance Report on the Observance of Standards and Codes (CG-ROSC) in 2004. The standards cover issues such as shareholder rights and ownership functions, equitable treatment of shareholders, role of stakeholders in corporate governance, disclosure, and transparency, and board responsibilities. The World Bank survey ranks 69 per cent of listed Thai companies as observing six key corporate governance standards set under the OECD. The remaining 31 per cent of Thai listed firms only partially observe the standards.

3. Standard Chartered Bank acquired 75 per cent of the equity and full management control of Nakornthon Bank and renamed it Standard Chartered Nakornthon Bank. In October 2005, Standard Chartered Bank, Bangkok Branch was integrated into Standard Chartered Nakornthon Bank, and the combined identity was named Standard Chartered Bank (Thai) Public Company Limited.

4. A deposit insurance corporation will be established in a few years' time to provide limited deposit insurance, unlike the current comprehensive deposit insurance provided by the government. Depositors will have to bear the risk related to each bank, and the government will no longer be stepping in to inject huge amounts of money to bail out troubled banks.

REFERENCES

Arrow, Kenneth J. "Social Responsibility and Economic Efficiency". *Public Policy* 21 (1973).

Bank of Thailand. *Supervision Report 2000*. Bangkok: Bank of Thailand, 2002.

———. *Supervision Report 2001–2002*. Bangkok: Bank of Thailand, 2000.

Booth, James R., Marcia Millon Cornett, and Hasan Tehranian. "Board of Directors, Ownership, and Regulation". *Journal of Banking & Finance* 26 (2002).

Borio, Claudia. "Towards a Macroprudential Framework for Financial Supervision and Regulation". *BIS Working Papers*, no. 128 (February 2003).

Brickly, J.A., J.L. Coles, and R.L. Terry. "The Board of Directors and the Enactment of Poison Pills". *Journal of Financial Economics* 35 (1994): 371–90.

Claessens, Stijn, Simon Dijankov, and Lary Lang. "Who Controls East Asian Corporations?" World Bank Policy Research Working Paper 2054. Washington, DC: World Bank, 1999.

Credit Lyonnais Securities (CLSA). *Ranking of Emerging Markets for Corporate Governance*. Hong Kong: CLSA Asia-Pacific Market, 2002.

Farma, E.E., and M.C. Jensen. "Separation of Ownership and Control". *Journal of Law and Economics* 26 (1983): 301–49.

Flannery, M. "Debt Maturity and the Deadweight Cost of Leverage: Optimally Financing Banking Firms". *American Economic Review* 84 (1994): 320–31.

La Porta, Rafael, Florencio Lopez-de-Silances, and Andrei Shleifer. "Law and Finance". *Journal of Political Economy* 106 (1998): 1113–55.

Litan, Robert E., Michael Pormerleano, and V. Sundarajan. *Financial Sector Governance: The Role of the Public and Private Sectors*. Washington: Brooking Press, 2002.

Saunders, A., E. Strock, and N. Travlos. "Ownership Structure Deregulation and Bank Risk Taking". *Journal of Finance* 55 (1990): 643–54.

Shleifer, Andrei, and Robert W. Vishny. "A Survey of Corporate Governance". *Journal of Finance* 52 (1997): 737–83.

3

Corporate Governance among State-Owned Enterprises in Thailand

Deunden Nikomborirak and
Saowaluk Cheevasittiyanon

Much has been written about the governance of private enterprises, but very little on the governance of state-owned enterprises (SOEs). This is surprising considering that state enterprises continue to contribute a significant share of the national gross domestic product (GDP) in many countries, in particular, developing countries where the markets are not truly open to private competition. In case of Thailand, state enterprises contribute to a quarter of the country's GDP. A probe into the governance of government enterprises is therefore long overdue.

The privatization trend has swept across the globe. Almost every country, large or small, most developed or least developed, has privatization on the list of its policy agenda. This is a result of increasing intolerance with inefficiencies that are inherent in most SOEs. The transfer of state ownership to private hands is expected to improve efficiency through the elimination of bureaucracy, mobilization of fresh capital, and superior supervision, and business acumen from private owners. Unfortunately, from experience, these improvements may not be forthcoming if competition or effective regulatory oversight is not in place. Privatization may lead to a deterioration in the quality of goods and services as private owners seek to cut costs, or to raise prices as they seek to maximize profits. Therefore, privatization is indeed not a panacea for the ills of SOEs.

In countries where rules and regulations have not been fully developed or the capacity to regulate is limited, state ownership of uncontestable markets may be superior to private ownership. It is easier to regulate government-owned enterprises as corporate information is much more easily accessible compared with private enterprises.

It is also easier to carry out social policies through a state enterprise than through a profit-maximizing private enterprise when universal service rules are not yet clearly established. That being said, state enterprises are, however, subject to two major downside risks — political intervention and state bureaucracy — which contribute to corruption and inefficiency. But there is much that can be done to reduce such risks, such as working towards greater transparency in key decision processes, holding executives accountable for their actions or allowing greater participation among stakeholders, and so forth.

This chapter seeks to examine the nature of governance in state enterprises in order to assess whether it contributes to or prevents the downside risks of SOEs — that is, political intervention and bureaucracy — and provides recommendations on how the governance can be improved. The first section describes the organizational structure of Thai SOEs, including corporate control and ownership, composition of the board, selection of the CEO, and renumeration schemes. The second section addresses key governance concerns surrounding directors and CEOs, as well as shareholders rights, fair trade practices, and so forth. The last section provides recommendations on how the governance of Thai SOEs can be improved.

1. Thai State-Owned Enterprises

1.1 General Information about State-Owned Enterprises in Thailand

State-owned enterprises, according to the Budget Procedure Act BE 2502 (AD 1959), are enterprises in which state agencies or enterprises own more than 50 per cent of the equity share. An SOE is subject to specific rules and regulations governing employment, compensation rates, performance assessment and incentive schemes, taxation and procurement procedures. In 2002 there were 77 enterprises that were regarded as SOEs by the official definition.[1] These enterprises generated a revenue of 1.46 trillion baht, equivalent to 26.71 per cent of Thailand's GDP, and employed 274,570 workers, or 13.7 per cent of all government employees and 0.8 per cent of the country's workforce. The combined asset of these enterprises was 4.64 trillion baht or 85.54 per cent of the GDP (see Appendix Table 3.1 for the details of each state enterprise). State enterprises in Thailand are engaged in capital-intensive sectors with a disproportionately high revenue share compared with the employment share. This is not surprising as most SOEs are involved in basic utility services such as telecommunication, transport, electricity, and water, all of which are capital-intensive. Figure 3.1 shows that SOEs in the energy sector contribute to the majority share in terms of revenue (64 per cent), followed by those in the transport, finance, and telecom sectors.

It is also noted that state enterprises in Thailand generate net profits each year. In 2002, SOEs contributed 61,000 million baht to the government coffers. Therefore, privatization is less about cutting government subsidies, than about mobilizing private capital for future investment and promoting greater efficiency in preparing for a more liberalized market.

In Thailand, privatization has been on the national policy agenda for the last two decades. But many attempts were thwarted by the tide of nationalism — in particular, after the 1997 financial crisis — and by strong resistance from the union.[2] Tainted privatization where individuals connected to the ruling power were able to secure large lots of the coveted shares in privatized SOEs or their spin-off enterprises did not help. Thailand nevertheless did pass the Corporatization Law in 1999, which made corporatization of state enterprises possible simply by a

Figure 3.1
Revenue Share of All SOEs by Sector

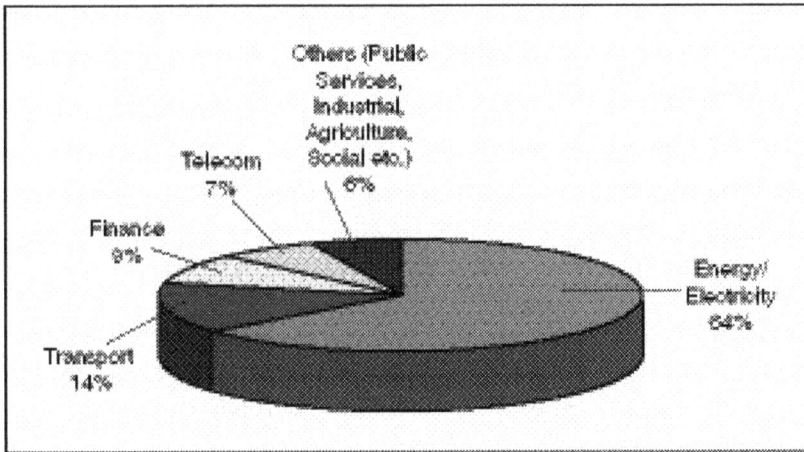

Source: Information Center, State Enterprise Policy Office, Ministry of Finance,
9 September 2003.

cabinet order without the need to amend the law which established it as a state enterprise. Thereafter, four state-owned companies have been corporatized since 2001: the Petroleum Authority of Thailand (PTT) in 2001, the Airports Authority of Thailand (AAT), and the Telephone Organization of Thailand (TOT) in 2002, and the Communications Authority of Thailand (CAT) in 2003. Three more state enterprises in the energy sector are expected to be corporatized and listed in the stock market in 2004. These include the Electricity Generating Authority of Thailand, the Metropolitan Electricity Authority, and the Provincial Electricity Authority.

1.2 Organizational Structures of State-Owned Enterprises in Thailand

1.2.1 Types of State-Owned Enterprises

There are two types of SOEs in Thailand: those that are incorporated and thus have a legal entity, and those that remain a government agency. Among the incorporated state enterprises, some are public companies while others are limited companies. There are six listed SOEs whose shares are traded in the stock market, namely, the Thai Airways International Public Company Limited (THAI), the Airports of Thailand (AOT),[3] the Krung Thai Bank Public Company Limited (KTB), the Petroleum Authority of Thailand Public Company Limited (PTT), the PTT Exploration and Production Public Company Limited (PTTEP), and the Bangchak Petroleum Public Company Limited (BCP). Two recently corporatized state enterprises are awaiting listing when privatization is due. These are the TOT Corporation Public Company Limited and the CAT Telecom Public Company Limited. Several state enterprises are limited companies, where the government maintains full ownership of the enterprise such as the Transport Company Limited, the Thai Maritime Navigation Company Limited, and the Aeronautical Radio of Thailand Company Limited. Most SOEs operate as government agencies, as shown in Appendix Table 3.1.

Indeed, those that are incorporated enjoy greater flexibility in the management of its enterprise.[4] However, the governance structure differs marginally between the two types of state enterprises as long as the government still holds a controlling share (Table 3.1). The only exception is that listed SOEs are subject to more stringent governance standards as stipulated in the Public Company Act BE 2535 (AD 1992) and the rules set by the Stock Exchange Commission of Thailand (SEC) and the SET. But even then, these enterprises are by no means free from political intervention and bureaucracy, perhaps just less so. The following are salient features of corporate governance among state enterprises in Thailand.

1.2.2 Corporate Ownership and Control

The shares of SOEs in Thailand are held by the Ministry of Finance (MOF). Their operations, however, come under the purview of the MOF relevant to the nature of the business in which each SOE is engaged. For example, the MOF owns shares in both the TOT Corporation Public Company Limited (fixed-line telephone operator) and the CAT Telecom Public Company Limited (long-distance operator). But the chairperson of the board of directors of both companies is the Permanent Secretary of the Ministry of Information, Communication, and Technology.

Table 3.1
Government Share Holding in Listed Companies, 2002

Name of Company	Government Shareholder	% of Total Share	As of
Transport sector			
Thai Airways PCL	Ministry of Finance	79.46	2 December 2002
	Government Savings Bank	13.39	
Finance sector			
Krung Thai Bank PCL	Financial Institutions Development Fund (FIDF)	87.27	11 September 2002
	Ministry of Finance	3.71	
	Government Savings Bank	0.79	
Energy sector			
PTT PCL	Ministry of Finance	69.28	10 April 2002
PTT Exploration and Production PCL	PTT PCL	62.84	31 December 2002
Bangchak Petroleum PCL	Ministry of Finance	47.87	05 April 2002
	PTT PCL	24.29	
	Krung Thai Bank PCL	1.73	
Ratchaburi Electricity Generating Holding PCL	EGAT	60.00	15 January 2003
	Government Savings Bank	2.62	

Sources: CD-ROM Listed Company Info 2002 (Q3–Q4) of the Stock Exchange of Thailand; Document 56-1 of the Stock Exchange of Thailand.

Nevertheless, one or two representatives of the MOF are present on the board of directors of each SOE.

1.2.3 Composition of Board of Directors

Boards of publicly listed companies are selected according to the Public Company Act BE 2535 (AD 1992) or the Civil and Commercial Code (Book 3: Specific Contract; Title 22: Partnerships and Companies) and thus have no pre-specified composition. The board of directors of each SOE that is a government agency is often appointed either by a minister of the relevant ministry or by the cabinet. There is no pre-specification of the board's structure, except that the executive director of each SOE is a director and secretary to the board. Ministers and the cabinet have the freedom to appoint any experts to the board. Politicians are not allowed to sit on the board, though their advisers are permitted to do so.

A typical board of directors of a listed SOE would consist of bureaucrats, academics, and the private sector. Bureaucrats normally occupy half of the board members with academics and the private sector occupying the remaining seats. The composition of the board of directors of the THAI is shown in Table 3.2. For state enterprises that are non-listed companies or government agencies, the composition of the board is very much dominated by bureaucrats with very few directors from the private sector or the academic circle, as is the case for the Electricity Generating Authority of Thailand (EGAT) shown in Table 3.3. Bureaucrats who often appear on the board of SOEs include the following:

- Representatives from the Ministry of Finance, who can be advisers to the minister, the permanent secretary (the highest-ranking bureaucrat in the ministry), the deputy permanent secretary, the director-general, or deputy-director of a department within the ministry, such as the Department of Excise Tax.
- Representatives from the ministry overseeing the particular business in which the state enterprise is involved, be it the Ministry of Transport, the Ministry of Information, Communications, and Technology or the Ministry of Defence.

Table 3.2
Composition of Board of Directors of Thai Airways International PCL

Board of Directors	Position
Dr Thanong Bidaya (Chairman)	Vice-chairman of the Economic Advisers to the Prime Minister (*political affiliation*)
Mr Srisook Chandrangsu (Vice-Chairman)	Permanent Secretary, Ministry of Transport Transport and Communications (*bureaucrat*)
Mr Somchai Engtrakul (Vice-Chairman)	Permanent Secretary of Finance, Ministry of Finance (*bureaucrat*)
Mr Thirachai Vudhidama	Adviser to the Chairman of Transport Committee (Senator) (*political affiliation*)
Air Chief Marshall Kongsak Vantana	Commander-in-chief, Royal Thai Air Force (*bureaucrat*)
Air Chief Marshall Terdsak Sujarak	Managing Director Airports Authority of Thailand (resigned May 2003) (*SOE executive*)
Mr Viroj Nuankhair	President Krung Thai Bank PCL (*SOE executive*)
Police General Sant Sarutanond	Commissioner-General, Royal Thai Police (*bureaucrat*)
Prof Dr Chai-anan Samudavanija	Director Vajiravudh College (*academic*)
Prof Dr Bowornsak Uwanno	Secretary-general King Prajadhipok Institute (*academic*)
Assistant Prof Dr Thatchai Sumit	President, Chulalongkorn University (*academic*)
Dr Olarn Chaiprawat	Director and Adviser to Management Board Siam Commercial Bank PCL (*private sector*)
Dr Vichit Surapongchai	Chairman of the Executive Committee, Siam Commercial Bank PCL (*private sector*)
Mr Chartsiri Sophinpanich	President, Bangkok Bank PCL (*private sector*)
Mr Kanok Abhiradee (Secretary)	President, Thai Airways International (*executive director*)

Source: Thai Airways International PCL (www.thaiair.com).

Table 3.3
Board of Directors of the Electricity Generating Authority of Thailand

Board of Directors	Position
Mr Choedpong Siriwich (Chairman)	Permanent Secretary of Ministry of Energy (*bureaucrat*)
Mrs Pannee Satawarodom	Director, Office of Debt Management, Ministry of Finance (*bureaucrat*)
Mrs Wannee Sampantarak	Secretary, Natural Resource and Environment Policy and Planning Office (*bureaucrat*)
Mr Somchai Wongsawat	Permanent Secretary of Ministry of Justice (*bureaucrat*)
Mr Sucharit Patchimnan	Director General, Department of Provincial Administration, Ministry of Interior (*bureaucrat*)
Mr Apai Jantanajulaka	Permanent Secretary of Ministry of Labour (*bureaucrat*)
Mr Prapat Potiworakul	President, Federation of Thai Industries (*private sector*)
Mr Pala Sukawet	Former Director, PTT PCL (*former SOE executive*)
Assistant Prof Lae Dilokwitayarat	Department of Economics, Thammasat University (*academic*)
Lieutenant Commander Wuttipong Pongsuwan	Adviser to the Ministry of Information, Communication, and Technology (*political affiliation*)
Mr Sittiporn Rattanopas (Secretary)	CEO, EGAT (*executive director*)

Source: EGAT (www.egat.co.th).

- Representatives from a law enforcement agency such as the Royal Thai Police, the Council of State, or the Office of the Attorney General.

Higher-ranking bureaucrats such as the permanent secretary of a ministry, director-general of an important department or the commander-in-chief of the police force or the military often occupy directorship in large state enterprises. Their deputies occupy seats on the board of directors of smaller state enterprises such as the Thai Maritime Navigation Co. Ltd. shown in Table 3.4.

Table 3.4
Board of the Thai Maritime Navigation Co. Ltd., September 2003

Name	Position
Mr Sommai Phasee (Chairman)	Deputy Permanent Secretary, Ministry of Finance (*bureaucrat*)
Police General Charnchit Bhiraleus (Vice-Chairman)	Deputy Commissioner-General, Royal Thai Police (*bureaucrat*)
Mr Boonyong Vechamanesri	Deputy Secretary, National Economic, Social and Development Board (*bureaucrat*)
Admiral Banawit Kengrian, Director	Chairman, Advisory Council of the Navy
Mr Wanchai Sarathulthat	Director General, Department of Maritime Transport and Navigation (*bureaucrat*)
Mr Mana Phatratham	CEO, Port Authority of Thailand (*bureaucrat*)
Mr Apisit Rujikeatkamjorn	Senior Executive Vice-President, Oil Business Group of PTT PCL (*private sector*)
Mr Suvit Chompoonutjinda	—
Mr Chotisak Asapaviriya	CEO, SME Bank (*SOE executive*)
Mr Nopporn Thepsithar	—
Lieutenant Commander Prarom Mokaves R.T.N. (Secretary)	CEO, the Thai Maritime Navigation Co. Ltd. (*executive director*)

Source: Thai Maritime Navigation Co. Ltd. (www.tmn.co.th).

1.2.4 Compensation and Incentive Scheme

Most SOEs do not have the freedom to set their own compensation rates for both employees and directors. These rates are set by the government. The salary ranges for employees of state enterprises are shown in Appendix Table 3.2. In practice, the enterprises are allowed to set the range of their own internal salaries as long as the maximum salary, which applies to the highest-ranking executive, does not exceed the ceiling rate. See Appendix Table 3.2. Each SOE has a different salary ceiling, depending on the size of its assets, revenue, profitability, the number of employees, which are assumed to be proxies of the scope of the responsibility of the particular chief executive officer (CEO). For example, the monthly salary of the CEO of the Fish Market Organization, a small enterprise, is capped at level 47 (at 62,080 baht), while that of the Telephone Organization of Thailand (TOT) is capped at the highest level — level 58 — at 100,920 baht. As for directors, the meeting honorarium is capped at 6,000 baht.

According to a study by Nikomborirak and Cheevasittiyanon (2002), these maximum salaries vary only marginally with the size of the SOE. This means that CEOs of large state enterprises, such as the TOT, are highly underpaid relative to the scope of their responsibilities. The same study also finds that due to the rigidity of the compensation scheme set by the government, SOEs are not able to offer competitive remuneration rates for professionals such as engineers, financial analysts, computer programmers, lawyers, and so forth. As a result, most SOEs often lack qualified professionals.

Recognizing that unattractive compensation may hamper the ability of state enterprises to attract qualified persons and therefore, their competitiveness, the government allows certain SOEs that operate in a competitive market and are financially sound to determine their own compensation and bonus scheme for their employees. These include all state enterprises that (a) are listed on the stock exchange, that is, THAI, KTB, and PTT; (b) display solid financial position, that is, the EGAT; (c) operate in a competitive environment, that is, Government Housing Bank (GHB), Export-Import Bank of Thailand (EXIM), Small and Medium Enterprise Development Bank of Thailand (SME Bank); (d) are specialized government agencies, that is, the Aeronautical Radio of Thailand Company Limited; and (e) are affiliated companies of SOEs. The wages and salaries offered by these state enterprises are comparable to those prevailing in the market. The study by Nikomborirak and Cheevasittiyanon (2002) shows that when comparing these rates to those

Figure 3.2
Comparison of Employee Compensation Rates Offered by SOEs and the Government

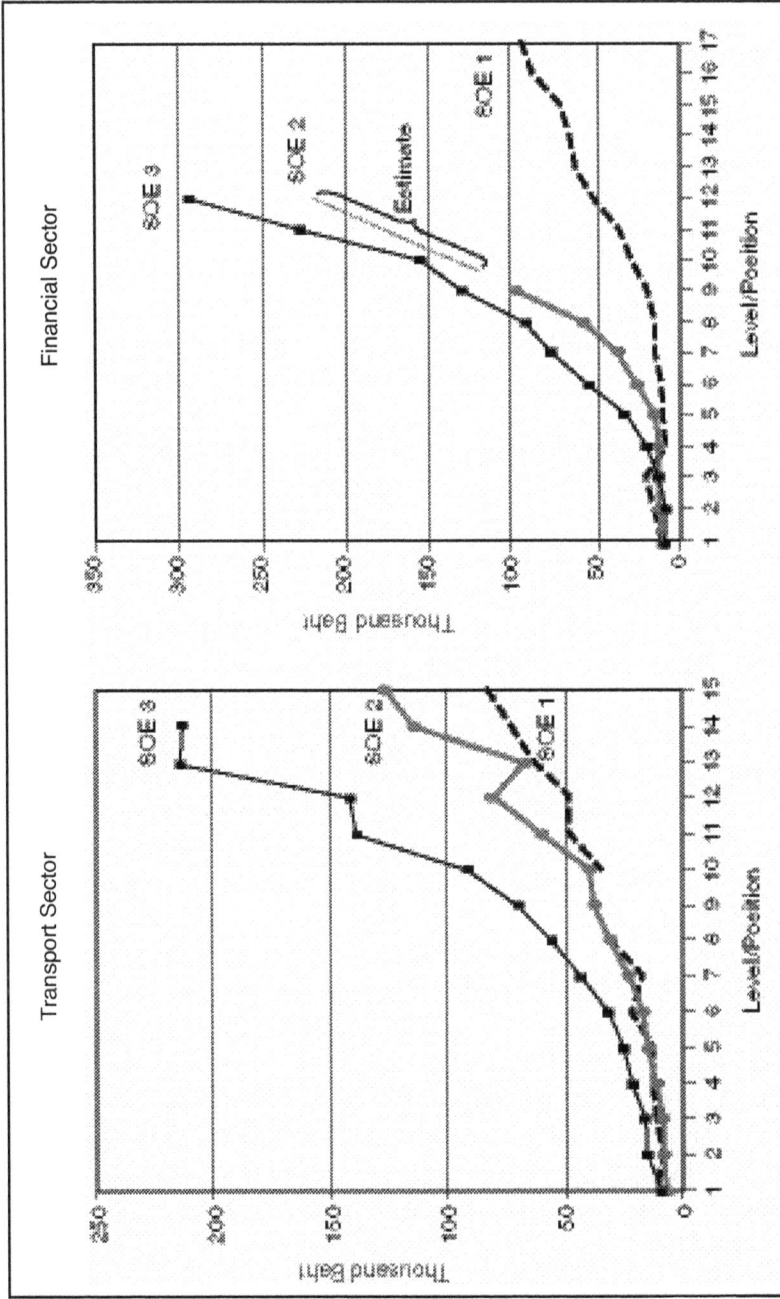

Notes
SOE 1: compensation rates determined by the government.
SOE 2 and SOE 3: compensation rates set by the state enterprises' boards.
Source: SOEs, April 2001.

prevailing in state enterprises that must adopt the rates pre-specified by the government, the gap is particularly large among high-level executive officers, as shown in Figure 3.2.

It is therefore not surprising that SOEs have a hard time retaining executives as well as professionals. For example, many high-ranking officers and engineers in the telecommunication sector left for cash-rich private telecommunication companies.

Another attempt to make the compensation more attractive was the adjustment to the remuneration package offered to CEOs. The revised package allows greater flexibility in setting the remuneration rate for CEOs based on performance (see more details in the next section).

The compensation rate for directors is equally unattractive. As mentioned earlier, the maximum remuneration for directors is capped at 6,000 baht (US$150) per meeting. But as in the case of employees' compensation, some SOEs are able to set their own rates. As can be seen in Figure 3.3, the remuneration rates for directors are significantly higher when the SOEs are free to determine their own rates, especially in the telecommunication sector, where competition for qualified directors is particularly fierce. While an easy conclusion can be drawn that the remuneration package for directors should be revised upwards, one must not forget that compensation should reflect the quality, the scope of responsibility, and accountability of the director. Therefore, as long as the selection of directors to the SOE boards is subject to political intervention and not based on merit, a revision of the compensation would not be justified.

It must be noted, however, that the directors of some SOEs are entitled to many fringe benefits, the costs of which are not properly calculated or disclosed. For example, until recently, every former and present director of the THAI and his family, that is, his wife and children under 25 years of age, are entitled to free air tickets. This privilege has been roughly estimated to cost the airline hundreds of million baht each year. Another collateral benefit for directors would be the privilege of sitting on the boards of affiliated companies, where directors' fees are not controlled.

Figure 3.3
Monthly Remuneration of Directors in SOEs and Private Enterprises

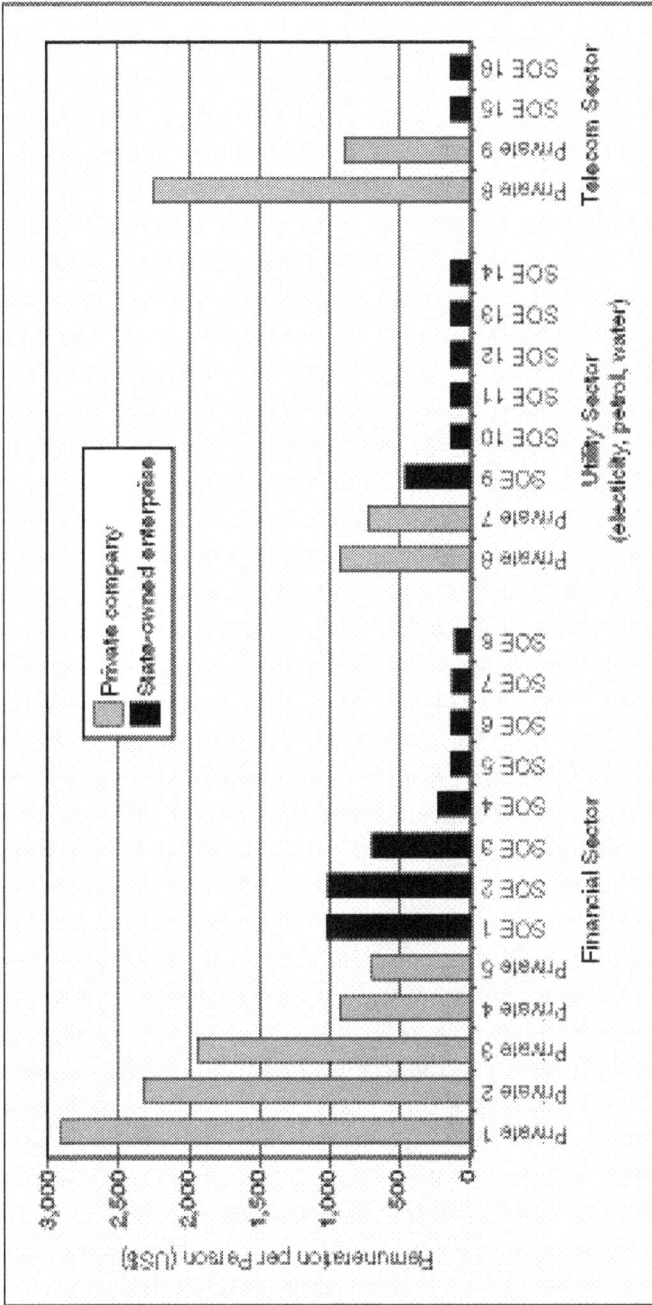

Note: The remuneration for directors on private companies' boards was calculated by dividing the total annual remuneration for the board by the number of months and the number of directors.
Source: Nikomborirak (2001).

1.2.5 The Chief Executive Officer

Before the revision of the Qualifications for Directors and Employees of SOEs Act in 2000, the CEO of a state enterprise will be an employee that has climbed the ranks within the particular SOE. He or she is likely to have spent many years with the enterprise and is familiar with its politics and management and is thus unlikely to assume the role of a "mover-and-shaker". Thus, to make it possible for SOEs to recruit professional managers that can initiate changes from outside, the law has been amended to allow CEOs to be sourced from inside as well as outside the enterprise. The board of directors is responsible for the selection of the CEO and the evaluation of his performance. The selected CEO will no longer be an employee of the particular state enterprise. Rather, he or she will perform his or her duty on a contractual basis with performance-based remuneration. This is seen as a first important step to shake up the traditionally dormant state enterprises, which are resistant to change — in particular, privatization. However, it is difficult for a CEO who is an outsider to manage the SOE without a team or without the cooperation of the employees.

Employees and directors of SOEs are also subject to an incentive scheme designed by the Ministry of Finance and approved by the cabinet. According to this scheme, the size of the annual bonus — calculated as a percentage of the enterprise's net profit — is determined by the result of the annual performance assessment. Several indicators reflecting various aspects of the enterprises including financial performance, quality of service, and level of efficiency are used to assess the overall performance.

While most large SOEs are enrolled in the incentive scheme, smaller ones prefer not to do so to avoid having to hire a private company to assess their performance each year as this is an additional cost. Those that do not participate in the scheme are still entitled to a bonus that is equivalent to 9 per cent of their net profits. This is why many profitable SOEs are content with a fixed bonus; they would rather not enter into a performance-based incentive scheme and risk receiving smaller bonuses if the enterprise's performance fell short of target.

SOEs that are loss-making but perform well are in fact "entitled" to a bonus. But they do not get any bonus as there is no fund allocated to bonuses from the budget. Considering that the profits generated by an SOE often reflect monopoly power and its losses, the provision of social services, rather than the level of its efficiency, the incentive scheme unfairly penalizes SOEs that provide social services in favour of those that are able to exploit their monopoly power.

2. Governance Issues

2.1 The Corporate Ownership and Governance Structure of SOEs

State-owned enterprises resemble widely owned enterprises in that everyone owns it — that is, all taxpayers — and yet no one owns it because the size of the stake is too small for an individual taxpayer to become involved in the supervision of the management and operation of the SOE. Unlike private widely held companies, however, state enterprises do have an intermediate shareholder that may act as a major shareholder — the Ministry of Finance. The Ministry may, on certain occasions, choose to exert its corporate control. On other occasions it may neglect its role as the intermediate owner (agent) of the ultimate shareholders (the principal), that is, taxpayers, by failing to effectively supervise and monitor management. Therefore, according to the authors' view, an SOE is unique in that it can be both a widely held company and a concentrated ownership company at the same time.

Widely held companies often suffer from the principal-agent problem. In the absence of a large shareholder, the management can easily take control of the company and abuse their power by rewarding themselves with high salaries, generous fringe benefits, a lavish retirement scheme and luxurious office and cars, and so forth. Companies with a concentrated ownership may not run into such a problem since major shareholders would oversee management to ensure maximum return on their investment in the company. However, the interests of major shareholders and smaller shareholders may not always coincide.

For example, if the major shareholder is interested in building a business empire, he may decide to channel the company's accumulated profits into acquiring new businesses rather than distribute the profits to shareholders as dividends. In the worst case scenario, the major shareholder may have the publicly listed company engage in business transactions, such as procurement, that would benefit his or his family's wholly owned businesses not listed on the stock market.

State-owned enterprises are prone to abuses by both the major shareholder — the government, who tends to see them as a political machinery — and by the management that tends to exploit them to secure private financial gains in the absence of effective owners' supervision.

Indeed, such corporate malaise can be prevented or lessened if the enterprise is managed in a transparent manner so that the board of directors can be held accountable for its decisions. The following sections examine whether Thai SOEs have the required structure and procedure to ensure good governance.

2.2 The Board

Unlike private enterprises, SOEs do not suffer from the domination of executive directors on the board. In fact, most SOE boards consist of only one executive director — the CEO. Other board members are outsiders, consisting of bureaucrats, academics, and executives from the private sector, as discussed earlier. State-owned enterprises perhaps suffer from too many outside directors that lack the necessary qualifications.

Firstly, many board members are simply representatives of different government organizations with little or *no knowledge or expertise* concerning the particular business in which the state enterprise is engaged. Moreover, these representatives are frequently replaced as a result of transfers, promotions, or restructuring within the particular government agency. Secondly, many board members have a *conflict of roles*. For example, the director of the Energy Policy and Planning Office, the current regulator of the energy sector, sits on the board of the PTT, the state petroleum enterprise listed on the stock market. Board members that represent the law enforcement agencies, such as the Royal Thai Police and the Attorney General Office, may also find themselves caught in a conflict of roles in case the SOE becomes entangled with legal issues. Thirdly, certain board members also have *conflict of interests*.[5] For example, the CEO of the TOT Corporation Public Company Limited — the fixed line telephone operator — is appointed to the Board of the CAT Telecom Public Company Limited, the long-distance telephone operator even when both compete indirectly in the cellular market.[6] Both also have a supplier-customer relationship as the CAT must access the TOT's local fixed line network and pay interconnection charges. Fourthly, while many directors on SOE boards are non-executive directors, they are *not independent* from politics. Most bureaucrats would always respond to the demands of politicians, that is, the ministers. While it is expected that the board must follow general policy directions set by the executive branch, it must be able to prevent corrupt practices, particularly in the procurement. A truly independent board must be free of influences by the management, politics, and business interests.

Finally, high-level bureaucrats, in particular permanent secretaries and director-generals sit on too many government committees. They also have full-time duties and responsibilities. They simply have *no time* to effectively perform a director's task. The Qualifications for Directors and Employees of SOEs Act BE 2518 (AD 1975) prohibits SOEs directors from sitting on more than three SOE boards.

The appointment of SOE board of directors has always been a political issue. This is because appointment to a state enterprise board, especially if the renumeration is very generous, is often viewed as a political favour. This is why a change in the government may at times lead to the appointment of an entire new board with new directors. At other times, a particular director appointed by the board may face strong resistance from employees and the union due to the lack of transparency surrounding the selection process. Some directors are looked upon as representatives of a particular politician sent to secure personal financial interests or to push forward a political agenda. The lack of the union's or employee's representation on SOE boards can lead to deep rifts between members of the board and the employees. Constant clash between the two can leave the SOE paralysed.

2.3 The CEO

As for the directors, it is not unusual for the public to suspect that the CEOs — especially those from outside the company — have often been selected on the basis of political connections rather than qualifications. As long as the selection process is not transparent and lacks participation from stakeholders, in particular a workers' representative, the CEO selected by the board or a committee set up by the government is unlikely to gain acceptance from employees. For example, the newly elected CEO on the board of the THAI was not welcomed by the employees, and the board was asked to disclose the reasons for having selected the particular CEO and the marks he received compared with other candidates. There was suspicion of political interference as there were rumours that the particular candidate had the support of those in power.

2.4 Transparency

The Public Information Act BE 2540 (AD 1997) stipulates that all government agencies must readily make available all information in their possession except those that are considered confidential private information or that concern or impinge upon national security. State-owned enterprises are obliged to disclose the terms and conditions of the concessions that they grant to the private sector. In practice, however, very few state enterprises make such documents available. One of the very few state enterprises that make available all concessions in its library is the TOT Corporation Public Company Limited. Its policy to make all concessions publicly accessible was adopted during the brief leadership of a CEO by the name of Mr Meechai Weerawaitaya, who believed in transparency. As concessions often involve large business stakes, they are frequently enmeshed in corruption, suspicions, and accusations. Thus, failure to disclose the details of such concessions would subject SOEs to speculations of corruption and vested interests.

Disclosure of the minutes of board meetings and related transactions and any conflict of interests among insiders — that is, the directors and executives — is not the norm. As minutes of board meetings are usually not available to the public, directors can rarely be faulted for their decisions. This is why scandals that revolve around the issue of connected transactions are commonplace for SOEs.

2.5 Equity

For the purpose of this study, the authors would like to define equity very narrowly, as the equality between small and large shareholders only. Those that concern other stakeholders, namely, consumers, suppliers, and competitors are examined below under the heading "Fairness".

An SOE that is wholly owned by the government should not have any equity problems, as the government is the sole owner of the enterprise. For those that are partially privatized, however — where the government continues to hold a majority share and the public a minority share — such problems are almost always inevitable. This is because, the government would often continue to run the SOE as an extension of the government rather than treat the privatized company as a profit-maximizing business entity. Government-mandated projects that SOEs are required to carry out may run against the interests of private investors that seek to maximize the return on their investment.

For example, a politician in the cabinet suggested that THAI opened a new route from Chiang Mai to Chittagong, Bangladesh, bypassing Dhaka, the capital. But there were concerns that the low passenger load would not be able to generate sufficient revenue to cover costs. It was also noted that to promote the route, a Thai consulate would have to be set up in Chittagong as visa applications are currently only available at the Thai embassy in Dhaka.[7] In such a situation, the board of THAI would have to carefully assess the profitability of operating the suggested route. If the expected revenues cannot cover the costs, then this has to be clearly highlighted. And if the opening of the route is to help promote bilateral tourism or trade, then an assessment has to be made to determine whether the expected gains outweigh the costs to be borne by the national airline. If so, THAI would have to be promptly compensated for the loss incurred from the operation, thereby protecting the interests of its small shareholders, the private investors. Failure to do so runs against the good governance principle of equity, where the interests of all shareholders, large and small, are to be equally protected.

Some countries also allow the government to hold a "golden share" in a fully privatized state enterprise, which will allow the government to veto any corporate decision with only a single share. A corporate control without ownership would likely translate to a lack of accountability on the part of the government as it does not suffer from the consequences of its decisions.

2.6 Accountability

Are the directors and the CEO of a state enterprise to be held accountable for their decisions and performance? As mentioned earlier, the CEO of a state enterprise is engaged in a fixed-term contract that provides for a performance-based remuneration package. Directors are also entitled to bonuses linked to the annual performance of the particular SOE, but these bonuses are insignificant. In general, the CEO, especially if he is an outsider, is subject to far greater scrutiny from the employees and the board of directors than directors are. Also, as board meetings are rarely properly recorded and disclosed, the decision-making process of SOEs remains unclear, and so directors can rarely be held accountable for their decisions.

2.7 Fairness

A state enterprise often holds a dominant position in the market. Many also wield regulatory power over private competitors.[8] Such a position of strength makes it all too easy for state enterprises to abuse its power and take advantage of suppliers, distributors, or customers to maximize profit for itself. This tendency to profit from an unfair advantage can be curbed by good governance.

Good governance includes fair trade practices, and SOEs should refrain from practices that would lead to a restriction of competition in the market. Measures to promote fair trade include (a) the imposition of anti-competitive clauses in concession contracts handed out to private operators; (b) the holding of shares in competing companies,[9] and (c) not over-pricing services in order to maximize profits.[10]

It should be noted that it is the regulator's role to ensure fair trade practices. Unfortunately, a full-fledged regulatory body has not yet been established in any of the service sectors that SOEs operate in: transport, telecommunications, energy, and water. Moreover, the Thai Anti-Monopoly Law or the Trade Competition Act BE 2542 (AD 1999) provides exemptions for state enterprises, which allows government-owned enterprises to wield their market power freely against competitors or consumers.

To briefly conclude this part of the chapter: SOEs face many governance problems, most of which can be attributed to the regulatory and political environment surrounding them. Political interventions lead to incoherence in SOE corporate strategy and management as members of the board of directors are frequently replaced. Such interventions also render state enterprises prone to corruption. Rigid rules and regulations mean that SOE hands are tied. However, the government has made several attempts to improve the environment in which the SOEs function, in particular the competitiveness of its remuneration rate for the CEO. Unfortunately, little has been done to promote greater transparency in the way in which SOEs operate and decisions are made. Most SOEs fail to comply with the Public Information Act; the selection of directors and CEOs are opaque; directors' perks and privileges as well as conflict of interests are not disclosed; and very few boards include an employees' representative or the union.

3. Recommendations

3.1 Directors and the CEO

The government is considering establishing a "directors pool" from which SOEs may look for qualified candidates. In this way, the selection of directors will be centralized and thus can be made more transparent. Even then, scepticism remains as to whether the central screening process will be free from political intervention. This will depend critically on the competition of the selecting committee. If politicians assume the chairmanship or occupy the majority of the committee members, or can exert their influence in the selection process, then no improvements can be expected.

To ensure that qualified directors and CEOs are elected, the authors would like to make the following recommendations:

- that the labour union or an employee representative is a member of the board and is involved in the selection process. Unlike the directors and the CEO who come and go, employees are permanently attached to the state enterprise and thus are more likely to be concerned about the long-term interest of the enterprise.
- that the board of directors set up a nomination committee that will collect and assess information regarding the qualifications and experiences of the candidates. The information should be disclosed to all employees as well as the public to ensure transparency.
- that all candidates declare any conflict of interests that they may

have had in the past until their application for the position. Failure to declare such interests may lead to disqualification or dismissal.

- that clear rules on how insiders — directors and executives — should proceed in case of a conflict of interests be established. This should, at the minimum, include a declaration of the conflict of interests not only to the board, but also to all employees, and the abstention from being informed about and involved in the decision-making process on the particular subject or issue.
- that individuals involved in the regulatory functions of the particular business in which the SOEs operate will be barred from becoming directors.

3.2 Transparency

Regardless of their legal status, all SOEs should try to adopt the disclosure standard applicable to listed companies, as stipulated by the SEC and the SET. This would include the requirement to disclose financial as well as non-financial information, connected transactions, as well as the auditor's full report. Also, as a state enterprise, the SOE is required to disclose all large-scale concessions and contracts that are of public concern and fringe benefits to which directors are entitled and had claimed.

3.3 Equity

To safeguard against possible political intervention of a privatized enterprise that may adversely affect the interest of private minority shareholders, partially privatized SOEs should always be compensated for loss-making projects mandated by the government. On this note, it is important that the SOE itself develops an effective accounting system so that the actual cost of implementing a government-mandated project can be estimated. However, if a privatized company is expected to maintain and fulfil its social mandate (fostering political ties), then the extent of the service obligations and the cost implications need to be estimated and disclosed to all investors beforehand.

3.4 Accountability

Directors, executives, as well as employees of the SOE need to be accountable to the ultimate owner — the taxpayers — for their performance. As mentioned earlier, the remuneration of the CEO is based on performance, with the assessment undertaken by the board of directors. As the directors (unlike the CEO) need to look at the longer-term goals of the enterprise, their compensation should not be dictated by the short-term financial performance of the SOE. Nevertheless, directors need to be accountable for their decisions. To promote greater accountability of directors, the minutes of the board meetings should be recorded in detail, with explanations and reasons for the decisions taken by the board and the views expressed by those on the board, in particular, of the minority vote.

The government-implemented performance assessment and incentive scheme needs to be fine-tuned and enhanced. Every state enterprise must be enrolled in the scheme to be entitled to bonuses. No SOE should be allowed to adopt a fixed-bonus scheme that disregards performance. The incentive scheme also needs to be "fair" to loss-making SOEs by allowing cost savings to be credited as available funds for bonuses. At the same time, the scheme should not emphasize financial indicators for SOEs that do not operate in a competitive market as that would encourage them to raise the charges of their services and abandon the provision of social services, which is their social obligation, the key rationale for their existence.

3.5 Fairness

To ensure that SOEs are not engaged in unfair or anti-competitive practices vis-à-vis their suppliers, competitors, distributors, and customers, all SOEs should subject themselves to the forces of competition. This would require an amendment of Section 4 of the Trade Competition Act BE 2542 (AD 1999). Even if the law does not currently apply to SOEs, the board of directors should always ensure that its trade practices do not violate the law. Also, to ensure fair competition, dominant SOEs that operate in a competitive market environment should relinquish their shares in competing companies.

3.6 Conclusion

To improve the corporate governance of SOEs, the government needs to change the approach in which it supervises and regulates these enterprises. It should free them from state bureaucracy and rigid rules and regulations. That is, it should abstain from "micro-managing" state enterprises by setting ceilings on the compensation rate, imposing rigid budgetary and procurement rules, controlling the number of employees, and so forth. The more the state becomes involved, the greater the risk of the SOEs becoming a government bureaucracy and thus subject to political interventions.

Indeed, greater flexibility must be balanced by greater accountability. Towards this end, the performance assessment scheme should be improved and the incentives strictly performance-based. Greater transparency through the disclosure of minutes of meetings, conflict of interests of insiders, remuneration of directors, and so forth, is a prerequisite for accountability. Without information, executives cannot be held accountable. A note of caution: a rush to permit greater flexibility without improvement in transparency and accountability would only subject SOEs to greater corporate malaise.

NOTES

1. Since enterprises with less than 50 per cent of government equity share are not considered SOEs, even if the government, as the single largest shareholder, maintains complete corporate control, the official number significantly underestimates the number of enterprises that are subject to state control. The 77 SOEs included 16 SOEs affiliated with the Financial Institutions Development Fund (FIDF) and subsidiaries of other SOEs, but do not include the Bank of Thailand (BOT) and the FIDF.

2. Labour unions are allowed in SOEs only. Some SOEs, such as the Electricity Generating Authority of Thailand, have a very strong union that would resist privatization.

3. AOT is formally known as Airports Authority of Thailand (AAT).

4. For example, an incorporated state enterprise can secure loans and sign contracts without having to obtain approval from the Ministry of Finance (MOF), its shareholder. Like a private company, it also pays a corporate income tax of 30 per cent instead of an annual contribution to the state coffers. The contribution is calculated as a percentage of net profits, whose figure may change from year to year depending on the decision of the MOF, rendering it unpredictable.

5. The Qualifications for Directors and Employees of SOEs Act bars SOEs executives

from holding positions in which there may be a conflict of roles or of interests with the SOE in which they manage, except in the case where the conflict arises out of duty. In particular, the law stipulates that SOE executives must not have held an executive position in private companies that are concessionaires, joint ventures, or that have other interests with the SOE within three years prior to holding an executive position in the concerned SOE. It is interesting to note that similar provisions for directors. So, SOE directors are not barred from sitting on the board of competing private enterprises or from holding shares in such companies. The only requirement is that the director must not sit on more than three SOE boards.

6. Both the TOT Corporation PCL and the CAT Telecom PCL independently hand out cellular concessions to private operators. Both earn a revenue share from their respective private concessionaires, which compete with each other in the market.

7. "Krongkasae Column", *Thaipost Newspaper*, 14 December 2002; "New Thai Route a Good Idea", *Bangkok Post Newspaper*, 21 December 2002.

8. For example, the telephone concession granted by the Telephone Organization of Thailand (TOT) prohibited private concessionaires from making tariffs adjustments without prior approval from the TOT, which competed directly with it.

9. For example, the EGAT continues to hold a large equity share in its spin-off company, the Ratchaburi Electricity Generating Holding PCL (Table 3.1).

10. The EGAT was criticized for implementing an automatic price adjustment formula that would shield itself from all risks, including fluctuations in the exchange rates, the price of procured electricity from independent power producers (IPPs), and small power producers (SPPs) and the level of demand in the market.

REFERENCES

"Krongkasae Column". *Thaipost Newspaper*, 14 December 2002.

"New Thai Route a Good Idea". *Bangkok Post Newspaper*, 21 December 2002.

Nikomborirak, Deunden. "The Role of Board of Directors". *TDRI Quarterly Review* 16, no. 3 (2001).

Nikomborirak, Deunden, and Saowalak Cheevasittiyanon. *Improving Incentive System and Compensation System of State-Owned Enterprises*. Bangkok: Thailand Development Research Institute, 2002.

Nikomborirak, Deunden, and Somkiat Tangkitvanich. "Corporate Governance: The Challenge Facing the Thai Economy". In *Corporate Governance in Asia: A Comparative Perspective*, pp. 407–22. France: OECD Publications, 2001.

Office of the State-Owned Enterprises and Government Securities, Ministry of Finance. *Good Governance Guidelines for State-Owned Enterprises*. Bangkok: Ministry of

Appendix Table 3.1

State-Owned Enterprises: General Information, 2002 (in Million Baht)

	Legal Status				Asset	Revenue	Net Profit (Loss)	Number of Employees
State-Owned Enterprises	Gov. Agent	Limited	Non-Listed	Listed				
Energy and Electricity								
1. Electricity Generating Authority of Thailand	x				382,086.13	215,730.90	27,350.33	27,950
2. Metropolitan Electricity Authority	x				94,349.29	93,694.24	4,677.97	10,386
3. Provincial Electricity Authority	x				175,498.32	150,554.41	5,491.83	27,965
4. PTT PCL				x	234,465.84	402,564.36	24,506.80	4,342
5. PTT Exploration and Production PCL*				x	81,745.13	31,692.45	12,088.95	749
6. The Bangchak Petroleum PCL				x	28,900.93	51,936.33	533.59	830
Total of Energy and Electricity					997,045.64	946,172.69	80,084.96	72,222.00
Transport								
1. Expressway and Rapid Transit Authority	x				156,851.82	8,150.42	830.42	3,892
2. State Railway of Thailand	x				70,326.85	8,212.04	(4,243.01)	16,540
3. Metropolitan Rapid Transit Authority	x				99,901.79	5,204.20	2,347.57	198
4. Bangkok Mass Transit Authority of Thailand	x				6,466.63	6,968.80	(3,271.61)	19,764
5. Transport Co. Ltd.		x			3,475.10	2,940.40	259.63	3,099
6. Express Transportation Organization	x				335.97	870.29	(32.76)	1,864
7. Port Authority of Thailand	x				24,797.61	6,197.71	1,711.73	4,196
8. Thai Maritime Navigation Co. Ltd.		x			319.25	159.17	17.02	51
9. Bangkok Dock Co. Ltd.		x			197.65	107.54	0.71	96
10. Airports Authority of Thailand PCL			x		41,121.69	34,440.31	1,690.09	2,761
11. New Bangkok International Airport Co. Ltd.		x			23,486.79	76.63	(374.86)	157
12. Thai Airways International PCL				x	178,231.65	130,276.98	10,181.92	25,520

			Revenue	Expense	Profit	Employees
13. Aeronautical Radio of Thailand Co. Ltd.		x	3,071.99	3,189.40	3.68	2,512
14. Civil Aviation Organization	x		593.16	303.39	24.72	225
Total of Transport			609,177.93	207,097.28	9,145.24	80,875.00
Telecommunication						
1. TOT Corporation PCL		x	284,064.15	64,089.54	21,478.70	22,006
2. CAT Telecom PCL		x	95,537.25	30,889.16	5,690.58	20,610
3. Mass Communications Organization of Thailand	x		4,774.26	1,737.58	664.53	1,066
Total of Telecommunication			384,375.66	96,716.28	27,833.81	43,682
Public Services						
1. Metropolitan Waterworks Authority	x		50,764.56	12,766.03	3,669.00	5,072
2. Provincial Waterworks Authority	x		41,141.62	7,498.81	277.16	6,017
3. Waste Water Management Authority	x		21.70	69.67	3.24	82
4. National Housing Authority	x		36,312.65	2,320.82	(976.35)	1,922
Total of Public Services			128,240.53	22,655.33	2,973.05	13,093
Industrial						
1. Thailand Tobacco Monopoly	x		16,839.58	41,124.16	4,958.92	4,817
2. Playing Cards Factory	x		193.36	150.48	48.97	526
3. Liquor Distillery Organization	x		840.41	344.70	94.41	198
4. Battery Organization	x		205.00	189.05	28.41	255
5. Tanning Organization	x		300.79	357.57	21.45	488
6. The Police Printing Press	x		270.28	102.56	13.24	122
7. Industrial Estate Authority of Thailand	x		12,750.73	2,784.20	1,004.90	583
Total of Industrial			31,400.15	45,052.72	6,170.31	6,989

Appendix Table 3.1 (continued)

State-Owned Enterprises	Legal Status				Asset	Revenue	Net Profit (Loss)	Number of Employees
	Gov. Agent	Limited	Non-Listed	Listed				
Agriculture and Natural Resources								
1. Forestry Industry Organization	x				2,901.78	1,269.03	14.00	2,011
2. Botanical Garden Organization	x				529.08	53.57	(29.00)	95
3. Dairy Farm Promotion Organization	x				992.15	2,265.00	(27.00)	1,195
4. The Marketing Organization Farmers	x				15,810.24	685.65	(35.42)	438
5. Thai Plywood Co. Ltd.		x			2,838.15	1,203.59	(158.71)	779
6. Fish Marketing Organization	x				970.84	295.00	3.35	336
7. Office of the Rubber Replanting Aid Fund	x				4,319.17	3,037.27	260.49	1,863
8. Rubber Estate Organization	x				607.30	491.32	54.73	452
Total of Agriculture and Natural Resources					28,968.71	9,300.43	82.43	7,169
Commercial and Services								
1. Government Lottery Bureau	x				10,684.39	2,825.68	517.73	829
2. Marketing Organization	x				145.86	745.32	8.58	65
3. Public Warehouse	x				857.71	1,099.04	30.87	415
4. Tourism Authority of Thailand	x				3,176.23	4,015.17	30.53	890
5. The Syndicate of Thai Hotels and Tourist Enterprises		x			239.11	25.22	20.88	2
Total of Commercial and Services					15,103.29	8,710.42	608.59	2,201
Social and Technology								
1. Office of the Public Pawnshop	x				1,881.13	263.70	107.10	366
2. Sports Organization of Thailand	x				2,466.01	1,058.14	(74.79)	526
3. Zoological Park Organization	x				1,895.59	47.15	(12.97)	587

4. Scientific and Technological Research	x	1,382.62	698.89	9.91	665
5. National Science Museum Site	x	1,291.21	109.15	7.64	78
6. Government Pharmaceutical Organization	x	5,300.79	3,384.43	505.82	1,935
Total of Social and Technology		14,217.35	5,561.46	542.71	4,157
Finance	x				
1. Krung Thai Bank PCL	x	1,058,387.95	46,908.78	8,009.16	14,653
2. Government Savings Bank	x	598,770.88	32,203.46	11,542.31	9,519
3. The Government Housing Bank	x	333,034.03	16,556.15	2,114.04	5,040
4. Bank of Agriculture and Agricultural Cooperatives	x	355,283.05	22,466.14	660.01	13,026
5. Export-Import Bank of Thailand	x	46,023.13	3,058.92	217.96	582
6. Small and Medium Enterprise Development Bank	x	12,336.08	657.11	83.69	630
7. Secondary Mortgage Corporation	x	1,907.55	105.06	1.53	47
8. Asset Management Corporation	x	29,384.97	5,248.44	2,419.92	557
9. Small Industry Credit Guarantee Corporation	x	5,025.12	340.04	(466.17)	128
10. Financial Restructuring Agency (FRA)*	x	767.81	18.12	(114.87)	—
Total of Finance		2,440,920.57	127,562.21	24,467.57	44,182
Total of SOEs (63 SOEs)		4,649,449.82	1,468,828.82	151,908.66	274,570.00

Notes
a. Total number of SOEs is 63 inclusive of one with PTT affiliation — PTT Exploration and Production PCL.
b. The Office of the Auditor General of Thailand approved only 44 financial statements of the SOEs.
c. * The FRA was omitted in 2002.

Sources
a. Information Center, State Enterprise Policy Office, as of 9 September 2003.
b. * Information from 56-1, Stock Exchange of Thailand.

Appendix Table 3.2
Compensation Rate Structure of SOE Employees since 1 October 1994

Step	Monthly Salary (Thai Baht)	Step	Monthly Salary (Thai Baht)	Step	Monthly Salary (Thai Baht)	Step	Monthly Salary (Thai Baht)
1	4,880	15.5	9,340	30	21,620	44.5	54,410
1.5	4,880	16	9,600	30.5	22,320	45	55,920
2	4,880	16.5	9,875	31	23,020	45.5	57,450
2.5	4,880	17	10,150	31.5	23,770	46	58,980
3	4,880	17.5	10,440	32	24,520	46.5	60,530
3.5	4,880	18	10,730	32.5	25,330	47	62,080
4	4,880	18.5	11,035	33	26,140	47.5	63,650
4.5	5,020	19	11,340	33.5	27,010	48	65,220
5	5,160	19.5	11,665	34	27,880	48.5	66,810
5.5	5,305	20	11,990	34.5	28,815	49	68,400
6	5,450	20.5	12,340	35	29,750	49.5	70,010
6.5	5,605	21	12,690	35.5	30,745	50	71,620
7	5,760	21.5	13,065	36	31,740	50.5	73,250
7.5	5,925	22	13,440	36.5	32,775	51	74,880
8	6,090	22.5	13,840	37	33,810	51.5	76,540
8.5	6,265	23	14,240	37.5	34,885	52	78,200
9	6,440	23.5	14,665	38	35,960	52.5	79,910
9.5	6,625	24	15,090	38.5	37,150	53	81,620
10	6,810	24.5	15,540	39	38,340	53.5	83,395
10.5	7,010	25	15,990	39.5	39,730	54	85,170
11	7,210	25.5	16,470	40	41,120	54.5	87,020
11.5	7,425	26	16,950	40.5	42,570	55	88,870
12	7,640	26.5	17,470	41	44,020	55.5	90,795
12.5	7,870	27	17,990	41.5	45,485	56	92,720
13	8,100	27.5	18,550	42	46,950	56.5	94,720
13.5	8,340	28	19,110	42.5	48,430	57	96,720
14	8,580	28.5	19,715	43	49,910	57.5	98,820
14.5	8,830	29	20,320	43.5	51,405	58	100,920
15	9,080	29.5	20,970	44	52,900		

Source: Information Center, State Enterprise Policy Office, Ministry of Finance, May 2001.

4

Thai Company Laws and Good Governance Practices of Unlisted Companies

Saravuth Pitiyasak

Since the 1997 Asian financial crisis,[1] the Thai government has launched a number of measures to reform corporate governance so as to restore investors' confidence and to speed up recovery from the deep recession. Those measures focus mainly on promoting good corporate governance practices in public listed companies. Not much attention has hitherto been paid to corporate governance among the unlisted companies. Nonetheless, it is undeniable that unlisted companies constitute the majority of the country's business enterprises and play a crucial role in the country's social and economic development. Hence, there is a need for research into corporate governance among the unlisted companies.

The aim of this chapter is to find appropriate solutions to strengthen corporate governance in unlisted companies in Thailand. The first section provides an overview of Thai company laws. This is followed by a comparative study of the statutory framework of corporate governance between Thai company laws and the Organization for Economic

Cooperation and Development Principles of Corporate Governance (hereinafter, the "OECD Principles") in Section 2.[2] Section 3 discusses the mechanisms for ensuring good corporate governance practices in Thai companies. The last section includes comments and recommendations for promoting greater corporate governance in unlisted companies in Thailand.

1. An Overview of Thai Company Laws: Statutory Framework of Corporate Governance

Thai company laws are composed of two pieces of legislation: one is the Thai Public Limited Companies Act 1992 (BE 2535) as amended by the Thai Public Limited Companies Act (No. 2) 2001 (BE 2544) (hereinafter, the "PCA"); and the other is the Thai Civil and Commercial Code, Title XXII, Partnerships and Companies (hereinafter, the "CCC").

1.1 PCA

The PCA is the law governing public limited companies or companies set up for the purpose of offering shares for sale to the public.[3] The liability of the shareholders of such companies is limited up to the amount paid on the shares owned.[4] In establishing a public limited company, 15 or more natural persons may act as promoters by preparing a memorandum of association and proceeding further in accordance with the PCA.[5]

Public limited companies include those that are listed on the Stock Exchange of Thailand (SET), called "public listed companies" and those that are not listed on the SET, called "public unlisted companies". The regulatory framework of corporate governance of public listed companies is subject to the PCA, the Security and Exchange Act 1992 (BE 2535) (hereinafter, the "SEA"), and other regulations under the SET and the Security and Exchange Commission (SEC) whereas that of public unlisted companies is subject to the PCA only.

1.2 CCC

The CCC is the law establishing and governing private limited companies. A private limited company is formed by seven or more promoters with its capital divided into equal shares and the liability of the shareholders limited to the amount, if any, unpaid on the shares respectively held by them.[6] The CCC also states that every promoter must subscribe for at least one share[7] and no invitation to subscribe for shares shall be made to the public.[8]

In the past, private limited companies could be listed on the SET, but in 1992 the SET announced that all private limited companies listed on the SET had to be converted into public limited companies by 16 May 1994. Because of this, at present private limited companies are not considered as listed companies on the SET. *Private limited companies seeking to be listed on the SET must be converted into public unlisted companies prior to applying to be public listed companies.*

2. Statutory Framework of Corporate Governance: OECD Principles Compared with Thai Company Laws

The OECD Principles cover five areas of good corporate governance: the rights of shareholders, the equitable treatment of shareholders, the role of stakeholders; disclosure and transparency; and the responsibilities of the board.

2.1 The Rights of Shareholders

According to the OECD principles, basic shareholder rights cover the right to participate and vote in general shareholders meetings; obtain relevant information on the corporation on a timely and regular basis; elect members of the board; and share in the profits of the corporation.

2.1.1 Participating and Voting in General Shareholders Meetings

Both the PCA and the CCC grant shareholders the right to attend and vote at shareholders meetings[9] and allow them to authorize other persons as proxies to attend and vote at any meeting on their behalf.[10]

Calling for an Extraordinary General Meeting: In addition to the right to participate and vote in a general shareholders meeting, Section 100 of the PCA allows shareholders holding shares amounting to not less than 20 per cent of the total number of shares or shareholders numbering not less than 25 persons holding shares amounting to not less than 10 per cent of the total number of shares to submit their names in a request directing the board of directors to call an extraordinary general meeting at any time.

Like Section 100 of the PCA, Section 1173 of the CCC also allows shareholders holding not less than 20 per cent of the total number of shares to request in writing to the board of directors to call an extraordinary general meeting. If the meeting is not called within 30 days, those shareholders or other shareholders holding not less than 20 per cent of the total number of shares may themselves call for it.

At present, a committee jointly appointed from the Ministry of Commerce, the Ministry of Finance, the SEC, and the SET (hereinafter, the "joint committee") is working on amending Section 100 of the PCA. In this matter, the joint committee views that the high requirement (shareholders holding not less than 20 per cent of the total number of shares or shareholders numbering not less than 25 persons holding shares amounting to not less than 10 per cent of the total number of shares) makes it difficult for minority shareholders to call an extraordinary meeting. Thus, the joint committee is of the view that the requirement on the total number of shares should be amended from 20 per cent of the total number of shares to 5 per cent of the total number of shares, without regard to the number of shareholders, so that minority shareholders holding shares amounting to only 5 per cent of the total number of shares would be able to call an extraordinary meeting. In this regard, the author agrees with the suggestion and views that the requirement under Section 1173 of the CCC should also be amended from 20 per cent of the total number of shares to 5 per cent of the total number of shares in order to align the CCC with the PCA.

Connected Transactions: Connected transactions or the buying and selling of assets between a company and its directors have sometimes been used to divert assets out of the company. This is unfair to minority shareholders, who have no control of the company. Section 87 of the PCA protects shareholders in the area of connected transactions by prohibiting any director of a public limited company to purchase the company's property or to sell property to the company or do any business with the company, regardless of whether this is done in his or her own name or in the name of other persons. Such deals shall not bind the company unless approved by the board of directors. Thus, a director of a public limited company is not allowed to purchase property belonging to the company or sell property to the company, or do any business with the company without the approval of the board of directors.[11]

Like Section 87 of the PCA, Sections 805 and 1167 of the CCC also imply that a director may not, without the consent of the board of directors, enter into a juristic act in the name of his or her company with himself or herself, or as agent of a third party.

To summarize, both the PCA and the CCC require that connected transactions be approved by the board of directors but do not require shareholders' approval, and thereby such transactions are the most common means by which corporate funds in Thailand are expropriated by majority shareholders who appoint the board of directors. In this regard, the author is of the view that the approval of shareholders rather than that of the board of directors be made mandatory for connected transactions (75 per cent of the number of shareholders attending the meeting who have the right to vote and who own shares not less than 50 per cent of the total number of shares).[12]

2.1.2 Obtaining Relevant Information on the Corporation on a Timely and Regular Basis

Section 101 of the PCA gives shareholders the right to obtain relevant information on the corporation on a timely and regular basis by requiring that before calling for a shareholders meeting, the board of directors prepare a written notice stating the place, date, time, agenda of the meeting and the matters to be proposed at the meeting, deliver it to the shareholders for their information at least seven days prior to the date of the meeting, and publish it in a newspaper at least three days prior to the date of the meeting.

Unlike Section 101 of the PCA, Section 1175 of the CCC only requires that directors either send the meeting notice to the shareholders not later than seven days before the date of the meeting or publish the notice at least twice in a local newspaper, not later than seven days before the date of the meeting.

The joint committee is of the opinion that the period of notification under Section 101 of the PCA should be amended from seven days to ten days to give the shareholder sufficient time to authorize someone else as proxy to attend and vote at the meeting on his behalf. The author agrees with this proposal and further views that the proposed amendment should be extended to Section 1175 of the CCC.

2.1.3 Electing Members of the Board

Section 70 of the PCA grants shareholders the right to elect directors by allocating to each shareholder the number of votes that is equal to the number of shares he holds multiplied by the number of the directors to be elected. The shareholder may choose to cast all his votes for one director, or any number of his votes to each of the directors.

Like Section 70 of the PCA, Section 1151 of the CCC has a provision for one or more directors to be appointed at the general meeting.

Removing a Director: In addition to the right to elect directors, Section 76 of the PCA stipulates that the shareholders meeting may pass a resolution to remove any director from office prior to retirement on account of the expiration of the director's term of office, by a vote not less than 75 per cent of the number of shareholders attending the meeting who have the right to vote and who hold shares not less than 50 per cent of the total number of shares.

Section 76 of the PCA makes it difficult for shareholders to remove a director because any resolution to remove him or her requires (a) not less than 75 per cent of the number of shareholders attending the meeting and (b) a vote of not less than 50 per cent of the total number of shares. The conditions are often found to be too restrictive, and the joint committee is of the view that this threshold should be relaxed to only require a vote of not less than 50 per cent of the total number of shares.

Like Section 76 of the PCA, Section 1151 of the CCC provides that a director can be removed by not less than 50 per cent of the number of voters present at the general meeting. Each shareholder present in person or represented by proxy shall have one vote, but on the poll every shareholder shall have one vote for each share of which he or she is the holder.

2.1.4 Sharing in the Profits of the Corporation

Both the PCA and the CCC grant shareholders the right to share dividends paid out of the profits of the company.[13] If the company still has an accumulated loss, no dividends shall be paid out.[14] Dividends will be distributed according to the number of shares held, with each share receiving an equal amount and the payment of dividends must be approved by a resolution passed at the shareholders meeting.[15]

2.2 The Equitable Treatment of Shareholders

Thai company laws ensure equitable treatment for all shareholders, including minority shareholders. All shareholders will obtain effective remedy for violation of their rights.

2.2.1 Revoking a Resolution

According to Section 108 of the PCA, shareholders of not fewer than five persons or who hold not less than 20 per cent of the total number of shares may request the court to revoke a resolution passed at a shareholders meeting which was in contravention of the article of association of the company or the provisions of the PCA.

Like Section 108 of the PCA, Section 1195 of the CCC stipulates that any shareholder may request the court to revoke a resolution passed at a general meeting which was in contravention of the article of association of the company or the provisions of the CCC.

2.2.2 Appointing an Inspector

According to Section 128 of the PCA, shareholders aggregately holding shares amounting to not less than 20 per cent of the number of shareholders or an aggregate number of not less than one-third of the number of shareholders may submit their names in a written application to the Registrar to appoint an inspector to proceed with the examination of the business operation and the financial condition of the public limited company as well as to inspect the business conduct of the board of directors.

Like Section 128 of the PCA, Section 1215 of the CCC states that shareholders holding not less than 20 per cent of the total number of shares of the company may apply for an appointment of one or more competent inspectors to look into the affairs of the company.

Nonetheless, even though shareholders have the right to appoint an inspector to examine the business operation and the financial condition of the company as well as the business conduct of the board of directors, an individual shareholder does not have the right to examine the books and records of the company's accounts or to request a copy of such documents. To provide greater protection for minority shareholders who have no control over the company, the author is of the view that there should be an additional provision in both the PCA and the CCC granting an individual shareholder the right of access to the details of the company's accounts.

2.2.3 Filing a Lawsuit against the Directors

Shareholders do have recourse against directors whose errant behaviour is damaging for the company whose shares they own. According to Section 85 of the PCA, shareholders who own 5 per cent or more of the total number of shares may issue a written notice directing the public limited company to file a lawsuit against directors found to be wanting in their duties as stipulated by the law, and whose actions would lead to damaging consequences for the company. If the company refuses to act, however, the shareholders may take the case to court and claim compensation on behalf of the company.

As for Section 85 of the PCA, Section 1169 of the CCC also stipulates that any shareholder may file a lawsuit against the directors for any injury they caused to the company if the company refuses to take the necessary action.

Nonetheless, whenever minority shareholders initiate a lawsuit and wins the case, all shareholders will stand to benefit from the successful action initiated by the minority shareholders. As the cost of the lawsuit is borne by the initiators of the case, there should be an additional provision in both the PCA and the CCC to allow the initiators of the lawsuit to seek a reimbursement of the amount incurred, with interest, from the company. This would be fairer to all as it removes the free rider problem.

2.3 The Role of Stakeholders

The OECD views corporate governance as covering the question of the stakeholders. According to the OECD principles, corporate governance means a set of relationships between a company's management, its board, its shareholders, and other stakeholders. Corporate governance also provides a structure through which the objectives of the company are set and the means of attaining those objectives and monitoring performance are determined.[16]

Like the OECD principles, the SET views corporate governance as covering the interests of other stakeholders by defining it as a set of structure and process of relationships between a company's management, its board, and its shareholders to enhance its competitiveness towards business prosperity and long-term shareholder value by taking into consideration the interests of other stakeholders.[17] Nonetheless, Thai company laws are quiet on the role of stakeholders. They do not include measures to protect other stakeholders such as employees, customers, suppliers, the community, the environment, and so forth. Legal protection of other stakeholders could be considered in other pieces of legislations such as the labour law, consumer protection law, and so forth.

2.4 Disclosure and Transparency

In order to protect the interests of shareholders, Thai company laws stipulate that the registration of a company must be made at the Company Registration Office, Ministry of Commerce, so that interested persons would be able to inspect or examine information about the company, that is, the objectives of the company, the shareholders' names and addresses, the articles of association, and so forth. In addition, directors of the company have the duty to register all new regulations, additions, or alterations, within 14 days of the date of amendment[18] or the date of special resolution.[19]

2.5 The Responsibilities of the Board

The PCA clearly provides that the directors are jointly responsible to the company[20] and the shareholders [21] for any clear violations of the rules of law. When it comes to the board's accountability to its fiduciary duty, however, the law is very vague. The PCA simply states that "in conducting the business of the company, the directors shall comply with all laws, objectives and the articles of association of the company, and the resolutions of the shareholder meetings in good faith and with care to preserve the interests of the company".

Like the PCA, the CCC has clearly spelt out the board's responsibility for clear violations of the rules of law, but it is vague on the board's accountability to its fiduciary duty. It simply asserts that the directors must in their conduct of the business apply the diligence of a careful businessperson.[22]

So, without fraud or a clear violation of the written rules and regulations, it would be difficult to prove whether a director has performed his duty in good faith and with care to preserve the interests of the company. The court has had little experience in interpreting such sections.

3. Mechanisms for Ensuring Good Corporate Governance Practices

3.1 Audit Committee

In January 1998 the SET announced that all public listed companies were required to set up an audit committee by December 1999 so as to increase the level of efficiency in its operations and to add value to the organization.[23] This is why at present all public listed companies in Thailand are required to have an audit committee.

Nonetheless, as there is no requirement in the PCA that public limited companies set up an audit committee, all public unlisted companies are free to decide whether they would set up an audit committee.

Like the PCA, the CCC does not require that private limited companies set up an audit committee to monitor the business operations of the management. Private limited companies are thus free to decide whether or not to set up an audit committee.

3.2 Independent Directors

Independent directors are appointed to safeguard the interests of minority shareholders, as minority shareholders usually do not have representatives on the board of directors. In Thailand, most public listed companies are controlled by majority shareholders, and therefore independent directors seem to be necessary to protect minority shareholders against any abuses of the management. In 1997 the SEC and the SET required public listed companies to appoint at least two outside directors who are independent of the major shareholders and the management. Independent directors have the duty of expressing their opinions on connected transactions and providing comments in the annual report.

Nonetheless, as there is no requirement for independent directors under the PCA, they are optional positions in public unlisted companies. Like the PCA, there is also no requirement for private limited companies in the CCC, and so private limited companies are free to decide whether or not to appoint independent directors.

3.3 Remuneration Committee and Executive Remuneration

One way of promoting transparency and accountability of the directors' remuneration is by using remuneration committees. In 1998 the SET initiated voluntary remuneration committees by recommending that all public listed companies set up a remuneration committee for determining executives' pay. A remuneration committee should be made up of wholly independent non-executive directors. Its objective is to enhance disclosures and accountability in executive remuneration. In addition, the present SEC disclosure requirement states that a public listed company must disclose the remuneration of the top 15 highest-paid management teams but in a lump sum amount.

But the PCA is quiet on the matter of remuneration committee and executive remuneration and so public unlisted companies are not required to disclose the remuneration of its management, or to set up any remuneration committee.

Like the PCA, the CCC does not require private limited companies to disclose the remuneration of its management or to set up a remuneration committee. They are free to decide on these matters.

3.4 Guidelines, Code of Best Practices, and Principles of Good Corporate Governance

3.4.1 Best Practice Guidelines for Audit Committee

In addition to requiring that public listed companies set up an audit committee, in January 1998 the SET established the best practices guidelines for the audit committee so that there is a clear understanding of the duties of the audit committee and the coordination required among the members of the audit committee, the internal auditor, and the external auditor.[24]

According to the guidelines, the audit committee must consist of at least three outside independent directors, each of whom should not directly or indirectly hold shares in the company amounting to more than 0.5 per cent of the paid-up capital.[25]

3.4.2 Code of Best Practices for Directors of Listed Companies

In December 1997 the SET issued its code of best practices for the directors of listed companies, the purpose of which is to ensure a high standard of management and to strengthen the confidence of share-holders, investors, and other related parties in the management of the company.

According to the code, directors are responsible for conducting their duties honestly; they are to comply with all laws, the objects and the articles of association of the company, and hold the resolutions of all shareholders meetings in good faith, and with care to preserve the interests of the company.[26] Moreover, directors are required to disclose in the company's annual report whether they have been in compliance with the code, and if not, the reasons for non-compliance.[27]

3.4.3 Guidelines for the Disclosure of Information on Financial Statements and the Summary Results of Business Operations of Listed Companies

The SET found that the financial statements of listed companies used for investment decisions by shareholders, general investors, and security analysts had provided insufficient information. So, in 1997 the SET issued guidelines for the disclosure of information on financial statements and the summary results of business operations of listed companies to ensure that listed companies provide sufficient information for investors to get a clear picture of their financial position.

3.4.4 Guidelines for Shareholders Meetings of Listed Companies

In 2001 the SET issued guidelines for shareholders meetings of public listed companies. This is to make sure that shareholders have sufficient information at hand for making decisions.

3.4.5 Principles of Good Corporate Governance

In 2001 the SET outlined 15 principles of good corporate govern-ance that public listed companies must set out with. Companies must demonstrate how they have applied those principles, along with reasons for non-compliance, if any.

Those 15 principles are: policy on corporate governance;[28] shareholder rights and equitable treatment;[29] various groups of stakeholders;[30] shareholders meetings;[31] leadership and vision;[32] conflict of interests;[33] business ethics;[34] balance of power for non-executive directors;[35] aggregation or segregation of positions;[36] remuneration for directors and the management;[37] board of directors' meetings;[38] committees;[39] a system of control and internal audit;[40] directors' report;[41] and investor relations.[42]

3.5 Good Corporate Governance Awards

3.5.1 Thai Rating and Information Service's
Corporate Governance Rating

The SEC has provided incentives for public listed companies to practise good corporate governance. In this regard, the Thai Rating and Information Services Company Limited (TRIS) has developed an internationally accepted system of rating corporate governance, which can be used as a measure of one's credibility standing.

Companies that have achieved satisfactory scores on the TRIS's corporate governance ratings will enjoy the following benefits. First, the SEC will grant companies with good scores a fast-track process for their initial public offerings of securities and reduce these companies' offering fees and annual fees by 50 per cent. The SEC will honour the companies by publicizing them on the SEC website. Secondly, the SET will reduce the companies' annual fees by 50 per cent. Finally, companies will get public recognition for their good governance practices.[43]

3.5.2 The SEC's Disclosure Award

As investors need information to make decisions, they will certainly value information disclosure. And to encourage public listed companies to continue to disclose information about their operations, the SEC rewards corporations that have an excellent information disclosure system. This award is to motivate companies to work within the guidelines so that they are comfortable sharing information about their company's operations. In 2002 there were 40 public listed companies that received the awards.[44]

3.5.3 Institute of Internal Auditors' Awards

The Institute of Internal Auditors of Thailand (IIAT) was set up after the Asian financial crisis with the aim of promoting strong internal audit and effective risk management. The IIAT began to grant Corporate Governance Best Practices and Audit of the Year Awards to companies with best practices and best audit committees. In the year 2002 there were six winners in six categories, namely, major corporations, SMEs, subsidiary companies, banks and financial institutes, state-own enterprises, and audit committee of the year.[45]

3.5.4 Institute of Directors' Board of the Year Awards

The Thai Institute of Directors Association (IOD) was established on 1 October 1999. It presents Board of the Year Awards to public listed companies guided by the corporate governance principles developed by TRIS. The criteria for the selection of the recipients for the Board of the Year Awards are based mainly on the management of each company's board of directors. The Board of the Year Awards were first given out in 2002, when eight public listed companies received the awards from the IOD.[46]

3.5.5 Thailand Productivity Institute's Best Practice Awards

The Thailand Productivity Institute was established by a resolution from the Thai cabinet in 1995. It is an independent agency whose objectives are to increase productivity and raise its standards in the industrial sector as well as the business community; increase the competitiveness of Thai industries in the global market; and to be the centre for coordinating and promoting productivity enhancement in Thailand.[47] In 2004 the Institute granted "Thailand Quality Class Award" to six companies.[48]

3.5.6 Q-Mark

There is at present a project initiated by the Thai Chamber of Commerce and the Federation of Thai Industries to award "Q-Mark" to companies (both listed and unlisted) with "good ethics".[49] Under this project, the goods and services of qualifying companies will receive a stamp of approval to certify the transparent and ethical quality of their corporate conduct. This will help improve the competitiveness of Thai goods and services in the international arena.

3.6 Training Programmes

The IOD works to raise the abilities of directors in Thai listed and unlisted companies to meet global standards and ultimately to strengthen the Thai economy. It serves as an education and policy centre for directors, and administers courses and certification programmes.[50]

3.7 Corporate Governance Centre

The SET has set up the Corporate Governance Centre to promote good corporate governance, to teach about the best practices guidelines, and to motivate listed companies to implement good governance principles.[51]

4. Promoting Greater Corporate Governance in Unlisted Companies

4.1 Current Situation

In Thailand, there are approximately 418 public listed companies,[52] 512 public unlisted companies,[53] and approximately 266,996 private limited companies.[54] Public unlisted companies and private limited companies are family-run businesses and their shareholding and management structure is concentrated within the family.

4.2 Problems and Their Significance

Of course, there are costs in practising good corporate governance. It appears that unlisted companies, mostly small and medium enterprises (SMEs), are less able than public listed companies to bear the costs of practising good corporate governance. At the very least, additional costs are required to set up an audit committee or to appoint independent directors. Besides the monetary costs, some companies are also concerned that "disclosure" may expose their trade information to their competitors.

Nonetheless, corporate governance is also of importance for unlisted companies, particularly those seeking to be listed on the SET, because in applying to be a public listed company, the companies may have to first show "good corporate governance" readiness. Not being able to do so may affect their application.

In addition, their adoption of "best practices" will win them favour in the eyes of banks, creditors, investors, strategic partners, as well as the top executive talent that such companies seek to recruit.

4.3 Comments and Recommendations

As discussed above, the focus has been to promote good corporate governance among public listed companies, with unlisted companies left out of the picture. A lot more thus needs to be done to promote corporate governance more widely to include the public unlisted companies and private limited companies.

The author takes the view that the achievement of greater corporate governance does not rest solely on the legal structure; rather, it also depends on the actual practices of company directors and management. Because of this, both regulatory and incentive measures to promote greater corporate governance in unlisted companies are required.

4.3.1 Revising Thai Company Laws

The provisions of the PCA and the CCC concerning the protection of the rights of minority shareholders, disclosure of information, and the responsibilities of management need to be revised.

Calling Extraordinary General Meeting: At present, Section 100 of the PCA and Section 1173 of the CCC, respectively, read:

> Shareholders holding shares amounting to not less than *one-fifth* of the total number of shares sold or shareholders numbering not less than twenty-five persons holding shares amounting to not less than 10 per cent of the total number of shares sold may submit their names in a request directing the board of directors to call an extraordinary general meeting at any time …

> Extraordinary meetings must be summoned if a requisition to that effect is made in writing by shareholders holding not less than *one-fifth* of the shares of the company …

After amendment, Section 100 of the PCA and Section 1173 of the CCC would read:

Shareholders holding shares amounting to not less than one-twentieth of the total number of shares sold may submit their names in a request directing the board of directors to call an extraordinary general meeting at any time.

Extraordinary meetings must be summoned if a requisition to that effect is made in writing by shareholders holding not less than one-twentieth of the shares of the company.

Connected Transactions: At present, Section 87 of the PCA reads:

Any director shall not purchase property of the company or sell property to the company or does any business with the company, regardless of whether it is in his or her own name or in the name of other persons. Such deals shall not bind the company unless approved by the board of directors.

After amendment, Section 87 would read:

Any director shall not purchase property of the company or sell property to the company or do any business with the company, regardless of whether it is in his or her own name or in the name of other persons. Such deals shall not bind the company unless approved by three-fourths of the number of shareholders attending the meeting who have the right to vote and who have shares totaling not less than half of the number of shares.

Unlike the PCA, the CCC does not contain a clear provision on connected transactions. Thus, an additional provision similar to the proposed Section 87 of the PCA should be added in the CCC.

Removing a Director: At present, Section 76 of the PCA reads:

The shareholder meeting may pass a resolution removing any director from office prior to retirement as a result of the expiration of the director's term of office, by a vote not less than three-fourths of the number of shareholders attending the meeting who have the right to vote and who have shares totaling not less than half of the number of shares held by the shareholders attending the meeting and having the right to vote.

After amendment, Section 76 would read:

The shareholder meeting may pass a resolution removing any director from office prior to retirement as a result of the expiration of the director's term of office, by a vote of shareholders attending the meeting who have the right to vote and who have shares totaling not less than half of the number of shares.

Examining the Company's Books and Records of Account and Requesting a Copy of the Documents: At present, even though the individual shareholder has the right to examine the minutes of proceedings, the resolutions of meetings,[55] and the register of shareholders,[56] as well as to request a copy of such documents, he or she does not have the right to examine the company's books and records of account, or to request a copy of such documents. To provide greater protection for minority shareholders who have hardly any control of the company, there should be an additional provision in both the PCA and the CCC granting an individual shareholder the right to examine the company's books and records of account or to request for a copy of those documents. The proposed provision would read: "A shareholder is entitled to examine the books and records of account of the company or to request a copy of such documents."

Filing a Lawsuit Against Directors: At present, minority shareholders who file a lawsuit against the directors of a company have no right to reimbursement from the company expenses. There should be an additional provision in both the PCA and the CCC giving minority shareholders the right to refund all expenses from the company. The proposed provision would read: "If any shareholder in bringing a lawsuit against the directors has made advances or expenses reasonably regarded as necessary, he or she may claim from the company a reimbursement of the principal with interest from the day it was made."

The Responsibilities of the Board: As mentioned earlier, it would be difficult to prove whether a director has performed his or her duty in good faith and with care to preserve the interests of the company, and the court has had little experience in interpreting such actions. Thus, there should be an additional provision in both the PCA and the CCC listing the non-exclusive circumstances that if found to be true, the director shall be deemed as having performed in bad faith and without care. The proposed provision would read:

A director shall be deemed as having performed his or her duty in bad faith and without care in the following non-exclusive circumstances:

(a) "Bad faith" shall be found when the director has entered into a connected transaction without shareholders' approval.

(b) "Bad faith" shall be found when the director, without shareholders' approval, has grant company loans to any person without collateral or adequacy of collateral.

(c) "Without care" shall be found when the director sits on too many boards that he or she cannot afford the time to properly monitor the management of the company.

(d) "Without care" shall be found when the director does not regularly attend meetings.

(e) "Without care" shall be found when the company's important or valuable assets or documents are destroyed or lost because of the negligence of the director.

4.3.2 Offering Incentives

Apart from revising the Thai company laws and related legislation, the author is of the view that providing incentives is an alternative to supporting good corporate governance in unlisted companies. Good corporate governance ratings should be an incentive for unlisted companies. Those winning high ratings should be rewarded. Both private and public sectors should provide incentives for eligible companies:

(a) Unlisted companies with good governance ratings should be entitled to a faster-track process and a reduction in listing fee if they apply to be listed on the SET.

(b) The SEC should cut securities offering fees for eligible companies, who will also enjoy privileged, speedier consideration processes when they submit plans for fund mobilization.

(c) The Ministry of Commerce (MOC) should award "best practices cards" to unlisted companies whose practices meet the criteria of good corporate governance. These companies should also get to enjoy corporate income-tax reduction,[57] faster value-added tax (VAT), and income-tax refunds from the Revenue Department.

(d) The MOC should set up a corporate governance centre to promote and encourage unlisted companies to see the importance and advantages of practising good corporate governance and to provide education and understanding about the best practices guidelines.

4.4 The Final Words

At the end of it all, the author hopes that good corporate governance practices will not be merely focused on listed companies. Unlisted companies also need to improve their corporate governance practices, as the issue of corporate governance is growing to be one of the major reasons cited for both domestic and international trade and investment. Also, the author hopes that this chapter will be an inspiration for academics, legal professionals, and law students to engage in broader and deeper exploration of this topic.

NOTES

1. The Asian financial crisis first arose in Thailand on 2 July 1997. It then moved to devastate Indonesia in October 1997 and it hit Korea in late November 1997. After that, the crisis went global to cripple the Russian economy, pressured Brazil's currency, and destabilized the Latin America economies.
2. OECD Principles of Corporate Governance (May 1999).
3. PCA, Section 15.
4. Ibid.
5. PCA, Section 16.
6. CCC, Sections 1096 and 1097.
7. CCC, Section 1100.
8. CCC, Section 1102.
9. PCA, Section 102, and CCC, Section 1176.
10. PCA, Section 102, and CCC, Section 1187.
11. In addition, SET rules require that if a public listed company has the intention of entering into any transaction with connected persons, the company must comply with the prescribed procedures. For example, if the volume of the transaction is not material, the company must disclose details of such transaction to the public, but if the volume of the transaction is substantial, the resolution from shareholders meeting must be obtained before entering into such transactions. In addition, in

calling a shareholders meeting to request for such transactions, the company has to provide an opinion of an independent financial adviser on the suitability of such transactions.

12. PCA, Section 107.

13. PCA, Section 115, and CCC, Section 1200.

14. PCA, Section 115, and CCC, Section 1201 para. 3.

15. PCA, Section 115 para. 2, and CCC, Section 1201 para. 1.

16. OECD, "Definition of Corporate Governance", www.oecd.org.

17. Stock Exchange of Thailand, "Report on Corporate Governance", August 2001, p. 9.

18. PCA, Section 40.

19. CCC, Section 1146.

20. PCA, Section 91, provides:
    The directors shall be jointly liable for any damage to the company in the following cases:

    (a) the calling for subscribers to make payment on share subscriptions or to transfer the ownership of the property to the company in a manner that does not comply with Section 37 or Section 38;

    (b) the spending of money for the payment on share subscription or the disposal of property received in payment for shares of the company in a manner that contravenes Section 43;

    (c) the performing of any act in contravention of Section 85.

21. The PCA, Section 94, provides the following:
    The directors shall be jointly liable for any damage to the shareholders and persons concerned with the company in the following cases, unless it can be proven that they had no part in such wrongdoing:

    (a) making false statements or concealing any information that should be disclosed about the financial condition and business operation of the company in the offer for sale of shares or debentures or other financial instruments of the company;

    (b) presenting or filling out a document submitted to the Registrar containing false information or particulars that which do not correspond to the accounts, registers, or documents of the company;

    (c) preparing a false balance sheet, a statement of profit and loss, minutes of a shareholders meeting, or minutes of a meeting of the board of directors.

22. CCC, Section 1168, para. 2.

23. SET, "Best Practices Guidelines for Audit Committees", p. 2.

24. Ibid., p. 1.

25. Ibid., p. 3. The audit committee's main duties are to: review the company's financial reporting process to ensure accuracy and adequate disclosure; review jointly with the external auditor and the internal auditor (if any) to ensure that the company has a suitable and efficient internal control system and internal audit; review the performance of the company to ensure compliance with the SEA, the SET regulations and related laws; select and nominate an external auditor; and prepare a report on its activities and disclose it in the annual report of the company.

26. SET, "The SET Code of Best Practices for Directors of Listed Companies" (19 January 1998), p. 1.

27. Ibid., p. 3.

28. The board should provide a report on the company's corporate governance policy.

29. The board should facilitate shareholders meetings in such a way that they encourage equal treatment for all shareholders.

30. The board should recognize stakeholders' legal rights (employees, suppliers, communities, rivals, and creditors, and so forth).

31. The chairman should allocate appropriate time and provide equal opportunities for shareholders to express their views.

32. The board should possess leadership, vision, and decision-making independence in the best interests of the company and the shareholders.

33. The board, the management, and shareholders should consider removing issues of conflict of interests.

34. The board should provide the code of ethics or statement of business conduct for all directors and employees.

35. The board, with approval from those at the shareholders meeting, has the duty to determine the number of directors, including independent non-executive directors.

36. The board and shareholders should be entitled to freedom of choice, with regard to the most appropriate way the company would go about the matter.

37. Remuneration for non-executive directors should be comparable to the general practice in the industry, with regard to work experience and commitment, as well as the benefits each director brings.

38. The board of directors' meetings should be scheduled to be held on a regular basis.

39. The board should enlist some committees, especially the audit committee and

remuneration committee, to help it study various issues in detail and screen the workload in particular situations.

40. The board should provide, maintain, and review a system in which financial operations and compliance controls are incorporated.

41. The board should indicate that it is its responsibility to prepare the financial statements, which are to be exhibited alongside the auditor's report in the company's annual report.

42. The board should ensure that the company discloses important information correctly, timely, and transparently.

43. Thai Rating and Information Services, "Corporate Governance Rating", http://www. tris.tnet.co.th/products_services/governance_eng.html.

44. National Corporate Governance Committee, "Disclosure Awards", http://www. cgthailand.org/SetCG/award/disclosure_en.html.

45. Institute of Internal Auditors of Thailand (IIAT), "Best Practices Awards", http:// www.theiiat.or.th.

46. They were Banpu Plc, Eastern Water Resources Development and Management Plc, Electricity Generating Plc, Thai Farmer Bank Plc, The Minor Food Group Plc, PTT plc, The Siam Commercial Bank Plc, and Tisco Finance Plc.

47. Thai Productivity Institute, http://www.ftpi.or.th.

48. Ibid.

49. National Corporate Governance Committee "Current Status", http://www. cgthailand.org/SetCG/status/status_en.html.

50. Thai Institute of Directors Association, http://www.thai-iod.com/eng/index.asp.

51. National Corporate Governance Committee "Mission", http://www.cgthailand. org/SetCG/center/center_en.html.

52. SET, "Market Statistics", http://www.set.or.th/static/market/market_stat.html.

53. Department of Commercial Registration, Ministry of Commerce, "Registration of public companies establishment and firms turning public (from the time of introducing the act up till 30 September 2005)", http://www.dbd.go.th/thai/ statistics/stat_m4.phtml.

54. Department of Commercial Registration, Ministry of Commerce, "Companies Registration, Dissolution and Survival (from the Time of Establishment of Registration Chamber up till 30 September 2005)", http://www.dbd.go.th/thai/ statistics/stat_m4.phtml.

55. CCC, Section 1207.

56. PCA, Section 63 and CCC, Section 1139.

57. Since 2002, corporate income tax has been offered to SMEs whose paid-up registered capital is less than 5 million baht. The tax rate for net profits up to one million baht is 20 per cent; net profits of between one million and three million baht will be taxed at 25 per cent; and profits of more than three million baht will be taxed at the usual rate of 30 per cent.

REFERENCES

Department of Commercial Registration, Ministry of Commerce. "Companies Registration, Dissolution and Survival (from the Time of Establishment of Registration Chamber up till 30 September 2005)". http://www.dbd.go.th/thai/statistics/stat_m4.phtml. 2005a.

———. "Registration of Public Companies Establishment and Firms Turning Public (from the Time of Introducing the Act up till 30 September 2005)". http://www.dbd.go.th/thai/statistics/stat_m4.phtml (accessed 31 October 2005). 2005b.

Institute of Internal Auditors of Thailand (IIAT). "Best Practices Awards". http://www.theiiat.or.th (accessed 31 October 2005).

National Corporate Governance Committee. "Current Status". http://www.cgthailand.org/SetCG/status/status_en.html (accessed 31 October 2005).

———. "Disclosure Awards". http://www.cgthailand.org/SetCG/award/disclosure_en.html.

———. "Mission". http://www.cgthailand.org/SetCG/center/center_en.html.

Organization for Economic Cooperation and Development (OECD). *OECD Principles of Corporate Governance*. http://www.oecd.org/dataoecd/32/18/31557724.pdf (accessed 31 October 2005). Paris: OECD, 2004.

———. "Definition of Corporate Governance". http://www.oecd.org (accessed 31 October 2005).

Official Gateway and Guide to Thailand for Investors. "Corporate Governance". http://www.thailandoutlook.com (accessed 31 October 2005).

Reid, Thelen, and Priest LLP. "Corporate Governance Reforms for Privately Held Companies". 3 September 2002.

SmartPros Editorial Staff. "CPA Warns Private Companies Can't Ignore Governance Issues". 20 June 2003. http://www.seminolebank.com/archives/2003/06/23.html (accessed 31 October 2005).

Stock Exchange of Thailand (SET). "The SET Code of Best Practices for Directors of Listed Companies". 19 January 1998. http://www.ecgi.org/codes/documents/ror_26_00.pdf (accessed October 2005).

————. "Best Practices Guidelines for Audit Committees". 23 June 1999. http://www.ecgi.org/codes/documents/ror_25_00.pdf (accessed October 2005).

————. "Report on Corporate Governance". August 2001. http://www.set.or.th/en/education/infoserv/files/CG15-ENG.pdf (accessed October 2005).

————. "Market Statistics". http://www.set.or.th/static/market/market_stat.html (accessed October 2005).

Thai Civil and Commercial Code, Book III, Title XXII, Partnerships and Companies (revised with effect from <?xml:namespace prefix = st1 ns = "urn:schemas-microsoft-com:office:smarttags"/> 1 April 1929).

Thai Farmers Research Center Co. Ltd. "*Enron* Lesson Stirs Movement toward Corporate Governance Promotion in Thailand". 25 March 2002.

Thai Institute of Directors Association. http://www.thai-iod.com/eng/index.asp.

Thai Productivity Institute. http://www.ftpi.or.th.

Thai Public Limited Companies Act 1992 (BE 2535) as amended by the Thai Public Limited Companies Act (No. 2) 2001 (BE 2544).

Thai Rating and Information Services. "Corporate Governance Rating". http://www.tris.tnet.co.th/products_services/governance_eng.html.

Urapeepatanapong, Kitipong. "Special: Shareholders and Their Rights". *Nation*, 9 June 2003.

Concluding Remarks

Sakulrat Montreevat

Good corporate governance is promoted nation-wide in Thailand. The Securities and Exchange Commission (SEC) and the Stock Exchange of Thailand (SET) have taken steps to help Thailand improve in this area as well as increase the efficiency of the Thai capital market.

Transparency and accountability to shareholders are the core elements for improving corporate governance. And there are regulatory and voluntary measures to ensure that companies listed on the SET observe them.

The voluntary approaches undertaken by listed companies cover board composition, guidelines for best practices, disclosure, protection of shareholders' rights, setting up committees to promote good corporate governance, education on good corporate governance, integrated marketing communication campaigns, awards and contests, research and monitoring studies on corporate governance, and corporate governance ratings. On the regulatory front, the authorities are looking into how some relevant legal instruments can be effectively used, for example, the Public Company Act, the new Securities and Exchange Commission Act, the Bank of Thailand Act, as well as bankruptcy laws.

It is recommended that Thailand's legal enforcement be intensified. The public should also be invited to lend their support to help the country develop a self-monitoring system. In addition, campaigns and other efforts to promote good corporate governance should be sustained for there to be any real lasting improvement in Thai corporate governance.

In the Thai banking sector, the Bank of Thailand (BOT) has issued guidelines on what constitutes good governance based on international standards. A survey has shown that the best governed banks in Thailand still lag far behind the average well-governed banks in Asia. Obviously a lot more effort is needed in this area to enable Thailand to measure up to international standards, for instance, more effective legal infrastructure could be put in place to ensure transparency, accountability, and fairness in the Thai banking sector.

As for state-owned enterprises (SOEs), efforts have thus far been focused on boosting efficiency rather than transparency. The governance and performance of SOEs can be further improved by raising standards of disclosure and assessing performance, as well as providing greater incentives to increase compliance. The carrot-and-stick approach on its own is insufficient to push SOEs to embrace good corporate governance.

Based on what has been observed internationally, Thai SOEs should be able to achieve effective corporate governance, given the correct institutional infrastructure as well as the right incentives to encourage the effort to switch to do the right thing. A clear separation of operations, policy, and regulation is probably the best option to ensure that SOEs are free from undue political interference to operate freely.

As for the unlisted companies, more reforms are needed. Even if they are guided by some standard of corporate governance, they lag far behind the listed companies in this area. Although no regulatory measures are imposed on the unlisted companies, they are strongly encouraged to take a look at some voluntary measures that they can apply to move towards good corporate governance companies. Progress in this has been slow, however, as the top concerns of unlisted companies are exposure of trading data and the cost of embracing good corporate governance. To address their concerns, the following could be considered: revising the company laws; setting up a corporate governance centre; and offering incentives. This will also redress the imbalance between listed and unlisted companies in Thailand.

Last but not least, there should be a study to analyse the costs and benefits of companies that have implemented good corporate governance in Thailand. Past surveys show a positive correlation between good corporate governance and company performance. But the findings need to be interpreted carefully because besides good corporate governance, there are also efficient management and other factors that can influence a company's performance.

Future research can continue from here to examine how corporate governance is practised in other ASEAN economies, and learn from each other.

Index

www.ingramcontent.com/pod-product-compliance
Lightning Source LLC
Chambersburg PA
CBHW021539260326
41914CB00001B/79